Who's Buried in Grant's Tomb?

Brian Lamb and the C-SPAN staff

Who's Buried in Grant's Tomb?

A Tour of Presidential Gravesites

with contributions by
Richard Norton Smith and Douglas Brinkley

PublicAffairs
New York

Excerpt from "Little Gidding" in FOUR QUARTETS, copyright 1942 by T. S. Eliot and
renewed in 1970 by Esme Valerie Eliot, reprinted by permission of Harcourt, Inc.

C-SPAN is directing all royalties from the sale of this book to the not-for-profit
C-SPAN Education Foundation. *C-SPAN, C-SPAN2* and *Book TV* are registered service marks of
the National Cable Satellite Corporation, d/b/a C-SPAN.

The information in this book has been carefully researched; however, locations and phone
numbers are subject to change. The publisher cannot take responsibility for changes.
Travelers are encouraged to call to verify information.

Written by Carol Hellwig with contributions by Anne Bentzel and Molly Murchie
Edited by John Splaine, Marty Dominguez, and Susan Swain
Book design by Ellen Vest; book layout by Donald Norwood
Photos by Brian Lamb
Original portraits by Chas Fagan

Library of Congress Cataloging-in-Publication data
Lamb, Brian, 1941–
Who's buried in Grant's tomb? : a tour of presidential gravesites / Brian Lamb and the
C-SPAN staff ; with contributions by Richard Norton Smith and Douglas Brinkley ; [written by
Carol Hellwig with contributions by Anne Bentzel and Molly Woods ; edited by Karen Jarmon,
John Splaine, Marty Dominguez, and Susan Swain ; photos by Brian Lamb ; original portraits
by Chas Fagan].
p. cm.
Originally published: Washington, DC : National Cable Satellite Corp., 1999.
Includes bibliographical references (p.).
PB ISBN: 978-1-58648-869-7
1. Presidents—Tombs—United States. 2. Presidents—Monuments—United States. I. Smith,
Richard Norton, 1953- II. Brinkley, Douglas. III. Hellwig, Carol. IV. Bentzel, Anne. V. Jarmon,
Karen. VI. Splaine, John. VII. Swain, Susan. VIII. Title.
E176.1 .L24 2003
973'.09'9—dc21
2002037026

To the memory of

Eric Clitheroe (1907–1986)
a great teacher

Bill Hartnett (1936–1980)
a true public servant

Cal Andringa (1941–1997)
a good friend

Contents

Contents

Foreword

Forty-Three Men and the Great Adventure

By Presidential Historian Richard Norton Smith

"And what the dead had no speech for, when living,
They can tell you, being dead, the communication
Of the dead is tongued with the fire beyond the
language of the living."

—T.S. Eliot

D o not believe the old axiom that dead men tell no tales. In truth, they comprise a virtual *Spoon River* of self-revelation. Not long before he died, Herbert Hoover chose a burial site on a gentle knoll in his boyhood home of West Branch, Iowa. Hoover gave instructions that nothing was to be built or planted that might obstruct the view between his final resting place and the tiny, 14- by 20-foot white frame cottage where his life began in August 1874. The old man wished to draw the visitor's attention to the two-room dwelling, its dimensions identical to those of the modern American living room. What Hoover *really* wanted to celebrate was the American dream, as embodied in the life of an Iowa blacksmith's son who would feed a billion people in fifty-seven countries, and serve one, mostly unhappy, term in the White House.

Even more reticent than the Quaker orphan from West Branch was his sphinxlike predecessor, Calvin Coolidge. No friend to pomp, Coolidge once observed that "it is a great advantage to a President, and a major source of safety to the country, for him to know he is not a great man." Consistent with this philosophy, he scornfully rejected the offer of a wealthy friend to build him and his family a gleaming marble mausoleum near the old homestead in Plymouth Notch, Vermont. Today the nation's thirtieth president lies beneath a plain granite headstone, alongside five generations of Coolidges, including the mother and son whose early deaths cast a permanent shadow across this shy, sentimental Yankee.

It was to Plymouth that I talked my parents into driving me in the summer of 1962, a few months before my ninth birthday. There, beneath the looming purple mass of Salt Ash Mountain, we discovered a toy village of six houses, a number unchanged since Coolidge was born at the back of his father's country store on the Fourth of July 1872. From this modest beginning grew a hobby that would strike others as only slightly less ghoulish than graverobbing. Classmates celebrated the Celtics and Bruins, deconstructed the lyrics of Lennon and McCartney, pulled trout out of local streams, or pasted stamps in a book. Some collected baseball cards. I collected deceased presidents. Dead men talking.

As a youngster of annoying precocity, I was entrusted with planning responsibilities for each summer's family vacation, thereby exposing my siblings to these and countless other gravesites, battlefields, and historic homes. My fellow passengers in this station wagon hell, immune to the thrill of the chase that motivates any true collector, took what consolation they could in each night's motel pool. The pursuit of underground history, so to speak, is not for the faint of heart, as we discovered one evening at the corner of Witherspoon and Wiggins Streets in Princeton, New Jersey. Twilight was falling; to prevent being locked in for the night, the family car was parked astride the cemetery gates.

In life a three hundred pound mountain of a man, in death Grover Cleveland is anything but conspicuous. Tracking my quarry by headlight beams, ten minutes went by. Fifteen. Twenty. Adding to the surreal tone of the hunt, who should I come upon but—Aaron Burr? As an unreconstructed Hamiltonian, I was tempted to do an impromptu jig on the old reprobate, but time was growing short, the night was growing dark and everyone in the car was growing nervous lest we be arrested for trespassing. Eventually a kind, if dubious, groundskeeper appeared, flashlight in hand, to point out the modest stone marker and urn that adorns the Cleveland plot.

Those who haunt cemeteries can sometimes put their own mortality at risk. As the nation's first dark horse presidential candidate in 1844, James K. Polk sparked little fervor ("James K. Who?" sneered rival Whigs who rallied to Henry Clay). Polk is still easily overlooked; on a broiling August afternoon in 1976, I contracted sunstroke while scouring a treeless expanse of lawn surrounding the Tennessee State Capitol in Nashville in search of the president who added more real estate to the United States than any other. *Sic transit gloria.*

Another youthful summer was spent in Ohio, a state which, as the self-proclaimed Mother of Presidents, is also the mother lode of presidential gravesites. By and large, chief executives from the Buckeye State demonstrate an inverse ratio between accomplishment in life and the lavishness with which that life is memorialized. (Of course, who would remember Cheops were it not for his pyramid?)

Consider Warren Gamaliel Harding. Nothing so became Harding's life as his leaving it. His messy death in a San Francisco hotel room in August 1923 led to journalistic speculation that his wife, Florence, had poisoned him. In the years since, a scholarly consensus has formed around the belief that she didn't, but should have. Today the Hardings rest unquietly on the outskirts of Marion, Ohio, condemned to an intimacy largely avoided in life, thanks to the generosity of countless schoolchildren who donated their pennies to construct a great hollow drum of white Georgia marble. Not far away is the famed front porch where Harding in 1920 proclaimed his desire for normalcy, and Mrs. Harding shooed away local mistresses whose desires ran in other channels.

Still another occupational hazard, a disappointed officeseeker, ended James Garfield's brief term in the summer of 1881. Angered over Garfield's refusal to give him the Paris consulship, Charles J. Guiteau shot the president in a Washington, D.C., railroad station. Guiteau had another motive for his crime: a frustrated author hoping to spur sales of his book, he anticipated today's tabloid culture, wherein notoriety is the surest ticket to a gig with Larry King (even if modern criminals generally wait until *after* committing an outrage to take the agent's call.)

In the feverishly inventive Gilded Age, even a mortally wounded president could inspire technological advance—in Garfield's case, the world's first indoor air conditioning system. Amid the stifling heat of a Washington, D.C., summer, a group of Navy engineers was summoned to the White House. Improvising a blower to force air cooled by six tons of ice through a heat vent in the president's sick room, they succeeded in lowering the temperature twenty degrees.

The patient remained snappish, hardly surprising given his diet of oatmeal and lime water. Told that the Indian warrior Sitting Bull was starving in captivity, Garfield snorted, "Let him starve." On second thought, a still more wicked alternative suggested itself. "Oh no," said Garfield, "send him my oatmeal."

Equally unrepentant, if decidedly more convivial, was Zachary Taylor, who declared on *his* deathbed, "I have no regret, but am sorry that I am about to leave my friends." It will come as no surprise that the same nineteenth century that reveled in gloom took a morbid interest in last words. Everyone recalls John Adams' poignantly inaccurate declaration of July 4, 1826, "Thomas Jefferson still survives." Less well known is Jefferson's political testament to his countrymen, contained in a letter published that very day in Washington's *National Intelligencer*. Gracefully declining an invitation by citizens of the capital to attend ceremonies commemorating the fiftieth anniversary of the Declaration of Independence, Jefferson reiterated his lifelong faith in the rights of man, and an optimism vouchsafed by "the light of science." To the end, he believed it a self-evident truth "that the mass of mankind has not been born with saddles on their backs, nor a favored few booted and spurred ready to ride them legitimately, by the grace of God."

Professing indifference over his ancestry, Jefferson took a much different view of posterity. The inscription he composed for his own granite obelisk listed authorship of the Declaration of Independence and Virginia's Statute for Religious Freedom, and his founding of the University of Virginia, to the exclusion of his service as the nation's third president. Andrew Jackson used characteristically blunter language to propel his parting shot. Asked if he had any regrets, the fiery Jackson replied, "Yes. I didn't shoot Henry Clay, and I didn't hang John C. Calhoun." More tenderly, Jackson admonished his family and servants, black and white, to keep the Sabbath faithfully. His last recorded words: "We will all meet in Heaven" (where, presumably, he didn't expect to encounter either Clay or Calhoun).

Jackson's great political rival, John Quincy Adams, lingered two days after a stroke felled him on the floor of the U.S. House of Representatives on February 21, 1848. Adams *did* meet Clay, his onetime secretary of state, with whom he enjoyed a brief, emotional reunion. "This is the end of the earth, but I am content," he is supposed to have remarked as breath ran out. It is a claim disputed by recent biographer, Paul Nagel, who points out, truthfully enough, that John Quincy Adams was never content. William McKinley, whose initial thought on being shot was for his assailant ("don't let them hurt him"), expired early in the morning of September 14, 1901, after calling for prayer and murmuring, "Goodbye, goodbye all. It is God's way. His will, not ours, be done." The earnest Grover Cleveland did not depart this life before reassuring history, "I have tried so hard to do right." At the last, a sightless Woodrow Wilson, the very picture of Scottish chill and Presbyterian rectitude, gasped a single word—"Edith!"—the name of his wife and White House protector.

It is no small irony that nineteenth-century presidents, for whom the Constitution existed as a limiting, not an enabling, charter, should have their graves marked by great piles of marble and stained glass, while their allegedly imperial counterparts of the modern era are entombed more modestly. Such is the contrast between Victorians who loved nothing better than a good prolonged cry, and the prosaic emotions of our ironic, if not cynical, age. A century ago, presidents were more remote but also more revered. To be sure, millions of Americans retain indelible memories of the untimely passings of Franklin Roosevelt and John Kennedy, but that was before twenty-four-hour-a-day exposure magnified the imperfections of our leaders.

Ever since George Washington was laid to rest "with the greatest good order and regularity" in December 1799, Americans have honored their deceased presidents with varying degrees of pomp and ceremony. As the first incumbent to die in office, William Henry Harrison was accorded a period of mourning scarcely shorter than his month-long tenure. By contrast, John Tyler's death in 1862 prompted a single paragraph notice, several days after the event, in Washington's newspapers. Such neglect may have been occasioned by Tyler's decision to throw in his lot with the Confederacy, in whose Congress he was serving at the time of his passing. In fact, well into the twentieth century, presidential funerals were essentially family affairs. Flamboyant in life, even Theodore Roosevelt went to his grave in a small cemetery near his beloved Sagamore Hill with admirable restraint. At his wife's request Woodrow Wilson was interred in the unfinished Washington Cathedral in February 1924, following a private service in the dead man's S Street home. The first president of the modern era to lie in state in the Capitol rotunda was William Howard Taft, and then for only ninety minutes prior to his burial at Arlington National Cemetery.

When Calvin Coolidge died three years later at his home in Northampton, Massachusetts, the ceremonies were appropriately minimalist. The strains of Handel's *Xerxes* filled a downtown church named for the Puritan divine Jonathan Edwards. President Hoover attended, as did Eleanor Roosevelt, the wife of the president-elect. Local stores remained open, their owners asserting, truthfully enough, that Cal would have wanted it that way. Washington limited itself to a memorial session of Congress. The wishes of the deceased carried less weight in 1945. Franklin D. Roosevelt's preference for a simple East Room service, with no embalming or lying in state, yielded to more elaborate pageantry consistent with his singular place in public affection and the history of his times. Hundreds of thousands of grieving citizens watched the president's caisson roll through the streets of Washington en route to Union Station. From there a funeral train carried FDR home to Hyde Park. A quarter century later Dwight Eisenhower became the last American president to ride the rails to his resting place, and the first to have his state funeral at Washington National Cathedral. Although the cathedral never realized its original objective as an American Westminster Abbey, it has become the *de facto* Church of the Presidents, at least for the ceremonial planners of the

Military District of Washington. Since Ike, the great Rose Window and soaring Gothic arches crowning Mount Saint Albans have twice provided a backdrop to presidential obsequies (Reagan in 2004 and Ford in 2007).

It is no accident that most recent presidents have chosen entombment at their presidential libraries, which are often located in settings that shaped their individual characters and outlook. Thus Harry Truman was buried a stone's throw from the office he frequented after leaving Washington (Truman especially enjoyed conducting tours of the library for visiting schoolchildren). His gravestone, inscribed with the seals of Jackson County, Missouri, the United States Senate, and the presidency, reads like a *Who's Who* entry, listing not only every office Truman held, but the dates of his marriage and the birth of his daughter. Andrew Johnson, with no library to commemorate his stormy tenure, insisted on being buried in an American flag, his head resting upon a copy of the Constitution whose wartime transformation he stubbornly refused to concede. Presidents, no less than historians, like to have the last word.

Then there was Lyndon B. Johnson, who chose burial in a family cemetery on the banks of his cherished Pedernales River, "where folks know when you're sick and care when you die." Two decades after Johnson received homage beneath the dome of the Capitol he had dominated as Senate majority leader and president, Richard Nixon passed up the formal commemoration of a capital city in which he had never felt at home. Emulating the example of his hero, Charles de Gaulle, Nixon opted for a less official, more heartfelt tribute in Yorba Linda, California—his Colombey-les-deux-Eglises. The town of his birth was also the site of his presidential library. As important, it epitomized the Silent Majority to whom Nixon had appealed during his time in the White House, and who turned out by the thousands to bid him farewell. In the interest of full disclosure: as one who had a hand in drafting Robert Dole's eulogy for Nixon, delivered on April 27, 1994, I will go to my grave convinced that Richard Nixon hoped to influence the 1996 presidential race from his. Should this really come as a surprise? An uncalculating Nixon, after all, is akin to a demure Madonna, nuance on talk radio, or a Unitarian pope.

In point of fact, Dole had been among the eulogists at Pat Nixon's funeral the previous June, as was California governor Pete Wilson. Both

Foreword

men were Nixonian favorites. Ten months later the audience was vastly larger as Dole and Wilson reprised their speaking parts, joined this time by President Clinton and Henry Kissinger. Approximately thirty-three million Americans watched Nixon's late afternoon burial in the lengthening shadow of his boyhood home. They saw a side of Bob Dole few would have predicted—except Nixon himself. For he knew that Dole's feelings lay just below the surface, much closer than his hardboiled public image suggested. As evidence, he had only to flash back to the lawn of the Russell County Courthouse in August 1976. Following his unexpected vice presidential nomination a day earlier, Dole had returned to Russell for what turned out to be a highly emotional homecoming. Looking out at the crowd on the courthouse lawn, he recognized old friends and neighbors whose spontaneous gifts to a post-World War II fund had enabled a badly wounded second lieutenant to undergo repeated surgeries on his shattered right arm and shoulder. As feelings of the moment mingled with gratitude for past kindnesses, Dole teared up.

In designating him one of his Yorba Linda eulogists, Nixon anticipated the sob in Dole's voice as he struggled to complete his tribute to the central figure in what the senator that day called the Age of Nixon. So authentic a display of grief was touching to all but the Nixon-haters in the vast audience. Moreover, by exhibiting his feelings so openly, Dole was, in effect, humanized in ways no other speech could have done. Which is exactly what Nixon intended, I believe, as he made his own funeral a showcase for his political heirs. Nixon was always a better campaign manager than candidate.

Nixon's modest headstone reminds onlookers that "the greatest honor history can bestow is the title of peacemaker." By going home to Yorba Linda, he joined a tradition as old as George Washington, and carried on by Jefferson, Madison, Jackson, Hayes, and FDR, each of whom rests on his ancestral acres. Less rooted, geographically and politically, was William Howard Taft, whose bumbling performance in the White House was redeemed by his later service as Chief Justice of the United States. Far more than the proverbially jolly fat man of most accounts, Taft was a thoughtful, wry observer of a world moving a bit too fast for his tastes. After finishing third in the 1912 election behind

Woodrow Wilson and Theodore Roosevelt, Taft said he consoled himself with the knowledge that no other American had ever been elected ex-president so resoundingly.

So mellow a figure would doubtless have chuckled over the complaint voiced by Herbert Hoover, on leaving Taft's 1930 Washington funeral service. When *his* turn came, remarked Hoover, he would see to it that mourners were not denied the pleasure of a good cigar.

The waspish Henry Adams asserted that it was easy to disprove Darwin's theory of evolution; all one had to do was trace the line of presidents stretching from Washington to Grant. Less jaded observers agree that the Grants, no less than the Washingtons, have much to teach us about a nation that is nothing if not a work in progress.

As Brian Lamb demonstrates in the pages that follow, there is no better way to personalize the past than through the lives, and deaths, of America's presidents. But then, I have long believed there is more drama in a graveyard than a textbook. Meanwhile, the true C-SPAN junkie is left to grapple with an existential question beyond any president's fathoming: Is there cable in Heaven?

A 1983 photo of Richard Norton Smith with former Boston Mayor Kevin White at the King's Chapel Burial Ground in Boston. They stand behind the gravestone of Massachusetts's first governor, John Winthrop.

Introduction

If you like to explore old cemeteries, take heart. You are not alone, as this book demonstrates. C-SPAN's guide to presidential gravesites is for people like you and me and historians Richard Norton Smith and Douglas Brinkley, who enjoy learning through personal experience and who think that, as historic sites, cemeteries have much to offer.

Why visit presidential graves? They are gateways to American history, helping us learn more about the men who held our nation's highest office and the times in which they lived. Americans believe our presidents are no greater than the rest of us. Nonetheless, only forty-three of our fellow citizens have made it to the White House and each helped shape the direction of our nation. When we learn about these men, we learn more about our collective selves.

If you're a curious but inexperienced gravesite tourist, don't be daunted by cemeteries. Presidential tombs are not morbid. The truth is, these graves aren't so much about death as they are about personal and political symbolism. In making this tour, I've come to realize how much presidents and their families, from our earliest times, understood the public nature of presidential deaths. Obvious care was given to planning most of their funerals and memorials.

Andrew Jackson and his beloved wife, Rachel, were buried under a cupola in the garden alongside their home in Nashville, surrounded by family members and Uncle Alfred, a favored slave. Our seventh president chose to have the title "general" chiseled into his sarcophagus. Thomas Jefferson also chose an epitaph that ignored his service as president. Visiting his iron-fenced grave at Monticello, you'll find him self-described for posterity as, "Author of the Declaration of American Independence, of the Statute of Virginia for religious freedom, and father of the University of Virginia."

Some of the presidents' final words can be as interesting as their epitaphs. William Henry Harrison, who served only one month of his term, seemed to have his place in history in mind while drawing his last breath. "I wish you to understand the true principles of government," he's reported to have said. "I wish them carried out. I ask nothing more." Grover Cleveland, succumbing to heart failure at age seventy-one, said, "I have tried so hard to do right." James Madison had no time to consider history. Expiring at the breakfast table, he tried to brush aside a niece's concern for his health, assuring her, "Nothing more than a change of mind, my dear."

Eight presidents died in office, four of them (Lincoln, Garfield, McKinley, and Kennedy) at the hands of assassins. Those who survived the White House lived anywhere from three additional months (James K. Polk) to more than thirty-one years (Herbert Hoover). The average age of our chief executives at death was seventy.

Quality of life after the White House varied greatly among the presidents. Many early presidents, like Grant, were virtually penniless. Worried about his family's financial future, the old general worked furiously on his memoirs while gravely ill with throat cancer. Thomas Jefferson sold his extensive book collection to the Library of Congress to support his life at Monticello. Harry Truman, our thirty-third president and a man of modest means, finally put presidential financial security to rest by successfully lobbying for a presidential pension.

Who's Buried in Grant's Tomb? is full of facts like these about the post–White House years of our presidents, their deaths, and their funerals. We also tell you how to visit each presidential gravesite, taking you to small towns and to several of America's largest cities. As you progress, you'll see ornate memorials from the Gilded Age and a few tucked-away plots in lesser known burial grounds.

The idea of gravesites as lessons in history was suggested to me by Richard Norton Smith, George Washington biographer and the former executive director of several presidential libraries. His foreword tells of his own childhood, spent visiting presidential graves with his sympathetic family in tow, and how this grew into a career as a historian. During a television interview about history, Richard commented to me that to truly understand something, one ought to try it for oneself.

Another historian who encouraged my experiential learning is Douglas Brinkley, who wrote the afterword for our book. Doug's an historian and Jimmy Carter biographer, and, at Rice University, has been known to pile his students onto a vehicle dubbed "The Majic Bus," to visit significant American cultural and historic sites. Doug is the kind of teacher who understands that personal experiences contribute to learning in ways that reading and lectures alone cannot.

Encouraged by the expeditions of these two historians, I began my own presidential gravesite tour in 1995, visiting and photographing thirty-six presidential graves and the libraries of the living former presidents over the next eighteen months. My journey began at Arlington National Cemetery, where two presidents are buried—John F. Kennedy and William Howard Taft, the only president to also serve as Chief Justice. Next was Washington's National Cathedral, where Woodrow Wilson lies beneath the stone floors of the church, in the style of the great European cathedrals. With a small touch of symbolism, I also ended my tour in the Washington area, visiting George Washington's burial site at Mount Vernon on a cold and quiet New Year's Day 1997.

Visiting the thirty-two other presidential gravesites in short order led to its share of adventures. In my initial days of grave-hopping, I planned a Hudson Valley swing, a triple-hitter, hoping to conquer the gravesites of Chester A. Arthur, Martin Van Buren, and Franklin Roosevelt in a single weekend. Arriving at the Albany airport on a Friday afternoon, I set out in a rental car for Albany Rural Cemetery where President Arthur is buried, only to find that the gates had closed at 5:00 p.m. I'd come too far to miss it. Spying no one, I decided to climb the cemetery's stone fence. Thankfully, I was able to find the grave, pay my respects, and snap a few photos without getting caught.

Readers of our book won't have to break any cemetery rules. *Grant's Tomb* gives detailed directions *and* visiting hours for every presidential gravesite. Those planning longer trips will find the memorials grouped by state in the appendix.

You will also find that many of the cemeteries on our presidential tour are filled with other interesting persons. In Cleveland's Lake View Cemetery, James Garfield has tycoon John D. Rockefeller, Ohio political boss Mark Hanna, and Lincoln assistant John Hay as his eternal neighbors. A stone's throw from Benjamin Harrison's grave in Indianapolis' Crown Hill Cemetery are three vice presidential resting sites—those of Thomas Hendricks (Grover Cleveland), Charles Fairbanks (Theodore Roosevelt), and Thomas Riley Marshall (Woodrow Wilson). A little additional exploration in these and other cemeteries will likely lead you to discoveries of your own.

Who's Buried in Grant's Tomb? was an outgrowth of C-SPAN's 1999 television series, *American Presidents: Life Portraits.* During this nine-month series, our cameras visited the birthplaces, gravesites, libraries, and family homes of the forty-one men who had then served as our country's chief executives. Hours of video about each president has been archived on our web site, www.c-span.org, along with biographical and historic details about each president and links to other sites.

Like our television series, this book was a collective effort by a number of people at C-SPAN. Carol Hellwig, now a former member of our executive staff, was the book's primary researcher and writer. With my tour and photos as her base, Carol spent months combing documents in the Library of Congress, reading presidential anthologies, and phoning cemeteries. Weeks of writing presidential death scenes, Carol reports, turned her into a uniquely interesting dinner table conversationalist.

Carol had assistance from Anne Bentzel and Molly Murchie, and from interns Megan FitzPatrick and Henrik Acklen. Lea Anne Long had two important roles in this project—arranging travel to each cemetery and organizing nearly one hundred rolls of film documenting the gravesites, created in a time before digital cameras were ubiquitous.

Our executive assistant, Amy Spolrich, helped with photo editing for this new edition.

Marty Dominguez was the overall coordinator of this book project, while Ellen Vest was responsible for its look. Initial editing was done by Karen Jarmon. Historical verification came from two sources—Richard Norton Smith, who made contributions to each chapter and checked our facts, and from longtime C-SPAN education consultant Dr. John Splaine. John contributed significantly to many of the historical projects mounted by our network. Susan Swain, our executive vice president, adds her indispensable work on this book to a long list of C-SPAN publications.

Thanks, too, to Peter Osnos, Susan Weinberg, and the rest of the staff at PublicAffairs. Their interest in this project allows this book to make its way to many new readers.

Finally, a word of thanks to the cable industry, especially our board of cable executives—this year, headed by Advance Newhouse Chairman Bob Miron—for their ongoing support of C-SPAN. More than thirty years ago, the cable television industry agreed to fund C-SPAN as a public service. C-SPAN is a not-for-profit company, offering commercial-free public affairs programming that includes daily live coverage of the U.S. Congress, programs about nonfiction books, extensive political coverage, and special series like *American Presidents*. Our affiliates, both cable and satellite, carry our three networks, C-SPAN, C-SPAN2, and C-SPAN3, as a service to their customers.

Who's Buried in Grant's Tomb? is a lighter look at American history, yet it has a serious intent. We hope our book, full of facts about the final years of our nation's chief executives, will send you on a journey of discovery that helps you better understand certain aspects of our shared national history.

Brian Lamb
Washington, D.C.
December 2009

The boast of heraldry, the pomp of pow'r,

And all that beauty, all that wealth e'er gave,

Awaits alike th'inevitable hour:

The paths of glory lead but to the grave.

—Thomas Gray, *Elegy Written in a
Country Churchyard*, 1750

George Washington

Buried: Mount Vernon Estate, Mount Vernon, Virginia

First President – 1789-1797

Born: February 22, 1732, in Westmoreland County, Virginia

Died: 10:20 p.m. on December 14, 1799, at Mount Vernon, Virginia

Age at death: 67

Cause of death: Sore throat

Final words: " 'Tis well"

Admission to Mount Vernon: $15.00

George Washington's election to the presidency was really more of a coronation. Every one of the sixty-nine electors voted for the leader whose resume read like a timeline for the new republic. Thus the commander in chief of the revolutionary army and president of the Constitutional Convention became the first president of the fledgling United States of America.

Washington served two precedent-setting terms in New York and Philadelphia, the new nation's first two capital cities. In 1797, Washington, a country squire at heart, happily retired with his wife Martha to their beloved Virginia estate, Mount Vernon. Having become an icon, he learned to cope with the constant stream of sightseers to his home. He lived to enjoy only three more years at his refuge on the Potomac.

A wintry mix of snow, sleet and rain pelted Mount Vernon on December 12, 1799. Washington made his daily inspection tour of the estate but came down with a sore throat the next morning. His condition worsened and by December 14 the general's throat began to close. Doctors were summoned.

Sign marking George Washington's first tomb. The bodies of George and Martha Washington were moved to a new tomb in 1831.

The dying Washington was in control to the end: afraid of being buried alive, he ordered his secretary, Tobias Lear, not to allow his body to be interred less than three days after his death. As he was taking his own pulse, George Washington died. He was sixty-seven years old.

Washington's final instructions were nearly ignored in the grief surrounding his death. A legacy-minded group sought to have his remains interred beneath the Capitol rotunda. To aid the cause, then Representative John Marshall secretly obtained congressional permission to have Martha Washington buried beside her husband. Ultimately, Washington's wish to rest forever at Mount Vernon was respected.

His hopes for a simple funeral were not as successful. The service included a long procession of mourners, a contingent from Washington's Masonic lodge, a band, and a military honor guard. Martha was given a quieter farewell when she died and was buried next to him in 1802.

Washington's will stipulated the construction of a new tomb to replace the deteriorating old family structure on the property. When that new vault was completed in 1831, the bodies of George and Martha Washington, along with those of other family members, were moved to their current location.

Touring George Washington's Tomb at Mount Vernon

Mount Vernon, owned and operated by the Mount Vernon Ladies' Association, is located sixteen miles south of Washington, D.C. It is open 7 days a week, 365 days a year. Hours are 8:00 a.m. to 5:00 p.m. April through August; 9:00 a.m. to 5:00 p.m., March, September, and October; and 9:00 a.m. to 4:00 p.m., November through February. Admission is $15.00 for adults, $14.00 for senior citizens, and $7.00 for children ages six to eleven. Children under six are admitted free. Special rates are available for groups.

From Washington: Take the George Washington Parkway south to Alexandria/Mount Vernon. Follow the parkway past Ronald Reagan National Airport, through Old Town Alexandria. Mount Vernon is eight miles south of Old Town, located at a traffic circle at the end of the parkway.

Mount Vernon is also accessible by bus and, in the summer months, by boat. Several sightseeing services also include Mount Vernon on their tours.

To find Washington's grave from the west side of the museum, follow the road (marked as "Tomb Road") directly to the grave.

For additional information

Mount Vernon
P.O. Box 110
Mount Vernon, VA 22121
Phone: (703) 780-2000
www.mountvernon.org

George and Martha Washington's final resting place

"'I die hard, but I am not afraid to go,' Washington informed his doctors." —Richard Norton Smith

Millions of tourists pay their respects before the red brick tomb whose construction George Washington had decreed in his will. Few making the trip to Mount Vernon have any idea of the theatrical scene enacted there in December 1799, by one of history's consummate actors. Taking charge of his treatment for a fatally sore throat, Washington held out his arm to be bled. "Don't be afraid," he assured his overseer. Over the next twenty-four hours or so, physicians would drain much of the old hero's blood supply. Around his neck, they placed flannel soaked in ammonium carbonate, a treatment no more effective than blisters of Spanish fly or vapors of vinegar. Heavy doses of calomel and emetick tartar emptied the patient's system of everything but the true source of his complaint.

Late on the afternoon of December 14, Washington asked his wife to go to his study and retrieve two wills from a desk there. One document was to be burned, the other preserved in her closet. As twilight fell, the ex-president seemed already to be wearing his death mask. "I find I am going," he told his secretary, Tobias Lear, adding that he faced the end "with perfect resignation." As thoughtful as he was organized, several times Washington apologized for the trouble he was causing. Lear, fighting back tears, said he only hoped to alleviate his friend's suffering.

"Well," replied Washington, "it is a debt we must pay to each other, and I hope when you want aid of this kind you will find it."

"I die hard, but I am not afraid to go," Washington informed his doctors. He felt his own fading pulse. The bedroom clock chimed ten as the dying man summoned his last reserves of strength. "I am just going," he whispered to Lear. "Have me decently buried, and do not let

Mount Vernon, Virginia

my body be put into the vault in less than three days after I am dead." (Washington wasn't alone in his dread of being buried alive; in her will Eleanor Roosevelt stipulated that her veins be cut as a precaution against the same fate.) The next morning saw the arrival of William Thornton, a family friend, amateur doctor and self-trained architect who had secretly designed the Capitol in the nearby Federal City as a final resting place for America's first president.

Never at a loss for ideas, Thornton proposed to resurrect the body laid out in Mount Vernon's handsome green banquet hall "in the following manner. First to thaw him in cold water, then to lay him in blankets, and by degrees and by friction to give him warmth, and to put into activity the minute blood vessels, at the same time to open a passage to the lungs by the trachea, and to inflate them with air, to produce an artificial respiration, and transfuse blood into him from a lamb." Other friends intervened to permit Washington a peaceful departure.

On Wednesday, December 18, Martha remained inside Mansion House as a little procession, led by the dead man's horse with its empty saddle, moved to the old family vault. A schooner anchored in the Potomac fired its minute guns and a Masonic band from Alexandria played a dirge. Local militia joined a handful of relations and friends in a brief service of committal. Later Martha consented to the removal of her husband's lead-lined mahogany coffin to Thornton's Capitol vault, on condition that she be allowed to share the space. Fortunately, the transfer was never made, thereby sparing the Father of his Country two centuries' exposure to lobbyists and boodlers.

In 1831 Washington's remains were moved a few hundred feet to the brick tomb that overlooks the Potomac. Having been embalmed while still living by a revolutionary generation in desperate need of a unifying icon, Washington of all people would understand why a million people a year are drawn to this place, hoping for inspiration with which to meet tests unimaginable to the Founders.

— RNS

George Washington

John Adams

Buried: United First Parish Church (Church of the Presidents), Quincy, Massachusetts

Second President – 1797-1801

Born: October 30, 1735, in Quincy, Massachusetts

Died: 6:00 p.m. on July 4, 1826, in Quincy, Massachusetts

Age at death: 90

Cause of death: Heart failure and pneumonia

Final words: "Thomas Jefferson still survives."

Admission to United First Parish Church: $4.00

In 1797, John Adams stepped into the historical shoes of the venerable George Washington. Though he succeeded a legend, Adams could lay claim to one notable "first" of his own: he was the first president to occupy the White House. He and his wife Abigail moved into the unfinished President's House, as it was then known, in the new capital city called Washington in 1800.

The second president had another distinction as well: he was the father and namesake of our sixth president, John Quincy Adams.

As president, John Adams had little trust in the masses; in truth, he was a political party of one. Defeated by Thomas Jefferson in 1800, Adams had more time for his solitary

George Washington biographer Richard Norton Smith at his subject's first resting place at Mount Vernon, Virginia, near Washington, D.C.

Historian Douglas Brinkley stands before a row of cenotaphs at Congressional Cemetery in Washington, D.C. The cemetery's receiving vault was a temporary resting place for several presidents. Historic figures buried there include Vice President Elbridge Gerry, Civil War photographer Matthew Brady, former F.B.I. Director J. Edgar Hoover and composer John Philip Sousa.

The original monument to the slaves of Mount Vernon, erected in 1929.

Fifty-six years later, this updated version was dedicated.

John Adams's tomb at United First Parish Church (Church of the Presidents) in Quincy, Massachusetts. Fifteen stars and stripes adorn the flag draped over his tomb, the standard design at the time of his presidency. Few flags like it remain—the original Star Spangled Banner is one of them.

ABOVE: James Madison was buried in the family cemetery on the grounds of his Montpelier estate in Orange County, Virginia. His monument towers over the other graves.

OPPOSITE: The cast iron fence enclosing Thomas Jefferson's cemetery at Monticello, Virginia. Jefferson's obelisk is visible to the right of the crest.

ABOVE: John Adams once told his son, "If you do not rise to the head of your country…it will be owing to your own laziness…." John Quincy Adams followed in his father's footsteps to become the sixth president. They are both buried in Quincy, Massachusetts at the United First Parish Church (Church of the Presidents).

OPPOSITE: James Monroe's Gothic tomb in Hollywood Cemetery overlooks downtown Richmond, Virginia.

Andrew and Rachel Jackson are buried beneath a cupola within sight of
the Hermitage, their 14-room plantation house near Nashville.

Marker for John Adams outside the crypt in Quincy's United First Parish Church (Church of the Presidents)

pursuits: leisurely walks and books. He retreated to the family home in Quincy, Massachusetts, where he harbored animosity toward his successor. For the next twenty-five years, Adams consumed the written word. When his eyesight failed and he could no longer read, he found others to read aloud to him. After a time, he renewed active correspondence with Thomas Jefferson. Though the two men had bitter political differences during their careers, they reconciled in retirement. Fate dictated that any distance between them would be bridged in death.

July 4, 1826 was an important day for the surviving founders—the fiftieth anniversary of the Declaration of Independence. Ninety years old and in failing health, John Adams declined all requests to participate in the holiday celebrations. Instead, he stayed home with his family. That afternoon, he lost consciousness and died of heart failure complicated by pneumonia. Adams's last words were "Thomas Jefferson still survives...." He had it wrong, however. Amazingly, Jefferson had himself died just a few hours earlier.

John Adams was buried alongside his wife Abigail at the United First Parish Church in Quincy, Massachusetts. President John Quincy Adams, his son, and wife Louisa were later buried at the same site.

Touring John Adams's Tomb at United First Parish Church

United First Parish Church (Church of the Presidents) is located in Quincy, Massachusetts, about ten miles south of Boston.

From Boston: Take Interstate 93 or Route 128 South. Take exit 7, onto Route 3 South to Braintree and Cape Cod. Take the first exit off Route 3 South, marked exit 18 for Washington Street. Continue on Burgin Parkway through six traffic lights. At the seventh light, turn right onto Dimmock Street. Go one block and take a right onto Hancock Street. The church is located at 1306 Hancock Street.

The church is also accessible via the Metropolitan Boston Transit Authority's subway system. From Boston, take the red line train to the Quincy Center station. Go right when exiting the train and continue up the stairs. Take a left at the top of the stairs and exit onto Hancock Street. The church is located at 1306 Hancock Street.

The Adams family graves are located in the basement crypt. To reach the crypt after entering the church through the main doors, take a right, go down the stairs, and take a left.

Guided tours of the crypt are also available for $5.00, beginning at the Adams National Historical Park Visitors Center, located at 1250 Hancock Street. The tour also includes the John Adams birthplace and the Adams family home. Tours operate from April 19 through November 10, from 9:00 a.m. to 5:00 p.m. Admission is $5.00, free for those under sixteen.

A view from inside the Adams tomb

For additional information

United First Parish Church (Church of the Presidents)
1306 Hancock Street (Quincy Center)
Quincy, MA 02169
Phone: (617) 773-0062
Fax: (617) 773-7499
www.ufpc.org

Adams National Historical Park
Visitors Center
1250 Hancock Street
Quincy, MA 02169
Phone: (617) 773-1177
Fax: (617) 847-3015
www.nps.gov/adam/

"Adams did not fear the great beyond."

—*Richard Norton Smith*

"*O*ld age is a shipwreck," mused Charles De Gaulle. For John Adams, the shoals came sharply into view in October, 1818, when his beloved Abigail, "the dear Partner of my Life for 54 Years and for many Years more as a Lover," died from typhoid fever. "I wish I could lie down beside her and die too," said the grieving husband. And what did he expect to find when his wish was granted? The ancient patriot told his son, John Quincy, that he had "the compatible prospect of dying peaceably in my own bed, surrounded by amiable and affectionate children, kind neighbors, and excellent friends." On the other hand, "I should not like to Live in the Millennium. It would be the most sickish life imaginable."

Having outlived his revolutionary contemporaries, Adams did not fear the great beyond. He quoted his old friend and sparring partner, Benjamin Franklin, who said, "We are all invited to a great entertainment. Your carriage comes first to the door: but we should all meet there."

The United First Parish Church, the final resting place for John Adams and his son John Quincy Adams

The carriage came for Adams on July 4, 1826. Not until 1891, however, was his crypt beneath Quincy's Unitarian church, now known as the Church of the Presidents or the Adams Temple, open to the public.

— *RNS*

John Adams

Thomas Jefferson

Buried: Monticello, Charlottesville, Virginia

Third President – 1801-1809

Born: April 13, 1743, at Shadwell, Virginia

Died: 12:50 p.m. on July 4, 1826, at Monticello, Virginia

Age at death: 83

Cause of death: Heart failure

Final words: "Is it the Fourth?"

Admission to Monticello:

November–February: $15.00

March–October: $20.00

The election of Thomas Jefferson as our third president in 1800 signaled the young nation's first move from republicanism to democracy. It was also a time of growth and exploration. When the new administration completed the Louisiana Purchase in 1803, the country doubled in size. Jefferson, always eager to explore new frontiers, sent Meriwether Lewis and William Clark on an 8,000 mile expedition through the western territory the following year.

Mostly satisfied with his accomplishments during his two terms, Jefferson retired to Monticello, his Virginia estate near Charlottesville. He was in debt and made a meager living from the sale of his crops. To maintain his genteel lifestyle, he eventually sold his 6,500 volume book collection to the Library of Congress for about $24,000. Despite his financial concerns, he devoted considerable energy to what would become one of his proudest achievements: the founding of the University of Virginia, which opened in 1825. Jefferson, the personification of the Age of Enlightenment, designed both the campus and curriculum.

Jefferson's presence was in demand on July 4, 1826. The holiday marked the fiftieth anniversary of the Declaration of Independence. Of the fifty-six signers, only three remained: Thomas Jefferson, John Adams, and Charles Carroll. Eighty-three-year-old Thomas Jefferson, feeling

Epitaph on Thomas Jefferson's grave, written by Jefferson himself

"weakened in body by infirmities and in mind by age," had declined all invitations to participate in the holiday festivities in Washington. On July 1, Jefferson began slipping in and out of consciousness. Jefferson had long suffered from rheumatism and an enlarged prostate and had regularly countered the pain with a concoction of opium and honey. During his last days, his doctor, Robley Dunglison, was on hand to administer the mixture, but Jefferson refused any medication. As though he were determined to hang on until the anniversary, Jefferson, in his lucid moments, asked several times whether it was the Fourth of July. With his family gathered at his bedside, Jefferson faded in and out of sleep. Finally, on July 4, he took his last breath; Dr. Dunglison pronounced him dead at 12:50 p.m.

As Jefferson had directed, an Episcopal rector conducted a simple graveside funeral service. He was buried in the family graveyard, next to his long-dead wife Martha, on the grounds of Monticello. The tombstone, Jefferson's own creation, noted his involvement with the Declaration of Independence, the Virginia Statute for Religious Freedom, and the University of Virginia. Jefferson left out his service as his state's governor and his nation's vice president and president.

Thomas Jefferson

John Adams, Jefferson's longtime political and intellectual sparring partner, also lost consciousness and died that same afternoon in Massachusetts. Adams's last words were "Thomas Jefferson still survives...." Unbeknown to Adams, Jefferson had died just a few hours earlier.

Touring Thomas Jefferson's Tomb at Monticello

Monticello is located off Interstate 64 near Charlottesville, Virginia. It is open daily except Christmas Day. Hours are from 8:00 a.m. to 5:00 p.m., March 1 through October 31, and from 9:00 a.m. to 4:30 p.m., November 1 until February 28. The Visitors Center is open from 9:00 a.m. to 5:30 p.m., March 1 through October 31, and from 9:00 a.m. to 5:00 p.m., November 1 through February 28.

Admission to Monticello is $15.00 for adults from November–February and $20.00 from March–October; it is $8.00 for children ages six to eleven year-round. Admission for children under six is free. Special rates are available for local residents and groups.

From Interstate 64: Take exit 121 to Route 20 South (if traveling westbound, turn left onto Route 20). Turn right at the first light to reach the Monticello Visitors Center. To reach Monticello, turn left on Route 53 just after the first stoplight. The entrance to Monticello will be on your right, about 1.5 miles from Route 20.

Jefferson's gravesite is located at the Monticello cemetery. To reach the cemetery after touring the house and grounds, follow the signs from the mountain top down Mulberry Row, heading west approximately 0.25 miles. The cemetery is at the end of that path. Visitors may also take the shuttle bus to the visitor's parking lot. Drivers stop at the cemetery, which is located about 0.3 miles from the lot.

For additional information

Monticello
Box 316
Charlottesville, VA 22902
Phone: (434) 984-9822
www.monticello.org

"'Nothing is better than a reliable friend,' wrote Jefferson." —*Richard Norton Smith*

All the DNA evidence in the world will tell you less about Thomas Jefferson than climbing his little mountain, where the philosopher who insisted that the earth belonged to the living made a poignant exception of an eighty-foot-square patch of blood-red soil just below its summit. "Nothing is better than a reliable friend," wrote Jefferson. Together with his closest friend, Dabney Carr, the future president concluded an adolescent pact under whose terms the survivor would bury his companion beneath a great oak tree on the mountainside. Carr enjoyed a meteoric rise through the colony's legal and political elite, marrying Jefferson's sister and establishing himself as a forensic rival to Patrick Henry.

Unfortunately, everything about Carr's life was to be premature, including death from bilious fever before his thirtieth birthday. Faithful to his promise, Jefferson moved the remains of his friend from their original grave to the hillside site hallowed by boyish memory. Simultaneously he calculated that at the rate the workmen prepared Monticello's graveyard, a single laborer could grub an acre in four days. It was vintage Jefferson, more precise than emotional—unless one credits the latest evidence of his long rumored liaison with Sally Hemmings, whose descendants have reasons of their own for seeking a place near Dabney Carr's oak tree.

— RNS

Thomas Jefferson's grave on the grounds of Monticello

James Madison

Fourth President – 1809-1817

Born: March 16, 1751, in Port Conway, Virginia

Died: June 28, 1836, at Montpelier, Virginia

Age at death: 85

Cause of death: Heart failure

Final words: "Nothing more than a change of mind, my dear."

Admission to Montpelier Estate: $14.00

He was a statesman best known as the "Father of the Constitution." Yet, had he lived in the modern media age, James Madison might never have become president. Our shortest president at 5'4", the soft-spoken Madison lacked the qualities of a successful politician. Luckily, his wife Dolley had enough for both of them. Attractive and outgoing, she made the White House the center of the capital's social circuit. While her husband led America to victory over Britain in the War of 1812, Dolley is remembered for saving George Washington's portrait from the burning White House.

James and Dolley Madison left the White House in 1817 after his two terms as president. They spent the next nineteen years at Montpelier, their estate in Virginia's Orange County. Even though he was one of the county's largest landowners,

Dolley Madison's grave at Montpelier

Madison had little money in retirement; a number of poor crops meant even less to live on. Yet he continued to contribute to the public discourse through debates on the slavery issue and through his involvement with Thomas Jefferson's University of Virginia. After Jefferson's death, Madison served as the university's rector until his own health began to decline.

During the first six months of 1836, James Madison was unable to leave his bedroom, his body plagued by a debilitating case of rheumatism. A neighbor of Jefferson's in the Virginia piedmont, Madison was treated by the same physician, Dr. Robley Dunglison, who tended to Jefferson in his final days. In his last months, clearly on the verge of death, Madison was told that drugs could prolong his life until the Fourth of July. He refused to try and delay the inevitable and thus did not survive to share the same memorable day of death as Presidents Adams, Jefferson, and Monroe.

Madison tried to eat an early breakfast with his family at Montpelier on June 28, 1836, when food lodged in his throat. One of his nieces grew concerned. Madison reassured her: "Nothing more than a change of mind, my dear." He then slumped over and died. He was laid to rest on June 29 in the family plot at Montpelier, an Episcopal priest committing his body to the earth. The funeral was attended by family, friends, and neighbors.

More than one hundred slaves looked on as the "Father of the Constitution" was buried.

After James Madison's death, his widow returned to Washington, where she lived out the rest of her years. She is buried next to her husband at Montpelier.

Touring James Madison's Tomb at Montpelier

From points north: Take Route 66 West to Route 29 South. At Culpeper, take Route 15 South. Continue on Route 15 to Orange. At Orange, take Route 20 South. Montpelier is located on Route 20 just four miles from the town of Orange.

From points south: Take Interstate 95 North to Route 64 West. From Route 64, take Route 15 North. At Orange, take Route 20 South. Montpelier is located on Route 20 just four miles from the town of Orange.

The Madison Family Cemetery is accessible via the Montpelier parking lot. Follow the marked path to the cemetery.

Montpelier is open daily except on Thanksgiving and Christmas. Hours are from 9:00 a.m. to 5:00 p.m. from April through October and 9:00 a.m. to 4:00 p.m. from November through March.

Admission to Montpelier is $14.00 for adults and $7.00 for children ages six to fourteen. Admission for children under six is free.

Note: You can no longer visit the cemetery without taking an official tour. The cemetery gates are only open to tour groups during visitor's hours.

For additional information

Montpelier
11407 Constitution Highway
Montpelier Station, VA 22957
Phone: (540) 672-2728
www.montpelier.org

"…Madison cherished hopes of freeing his slaves upon his death." —*Richard Norton Smith*

"*T*ake care of me when dead," Thomas Jefferson wrote James Madison, in February 1826, "and be assured that I shall leave with you my last affections." Faithful as ever, Madison succeeded his old friend as rector of the infant University of Virginia. Condemning southern nullifiers, he organized his voluminous notes on the Constitutional Convention for posthumous publication and cherished hopes of freeing his slaves upon his death. Madison was forced to abandon these plans as Montpelier sank into debt; idealism fell victim to the plantation economy (in his will, he did make modest provision for the American Colonization Society and its agenda of returning America's slaves to their African roots.)

The day after his death, the former president was buried in the Madison family plot half a mile south of his mansion. His much loved wife, Dolley, lived on in the nation's capital until 1849, sending the second telegraph (after Samuel Morse's immortal "What hath God wrought?") and being voted an unprecedented honorary seat in the House of Representatives. Her funeral was the largest Washington had ever seen, attended by, among others, "The Presidential Cabinet, The Diplomatic Corps, Members of the Senate and the House of Representatives…and their officers; Judges of the Supreme Court and Courts of the District and their officers; Officers of the Army and Navy; the Mayor and Corporation of Washington"—and a vast assembly of "Citizens and Strangers" come to pay respects to one of America's great women.

Originally laid to rest in the Congressional Cemetery on Capitol Hill, Dolley was not reunited with her husband until 1858. Today they sleep in the rolling horse country of Orange County.

—RNS

James Monroe

Buried: Hollywood Cemetery, Richmond, Virginia

Fifth President – 1817-1825

Born: April 28, 1758, in Westmoreland County, Virginia

Died: 3:15 p.m. on July 4, 1831, in New York, New York

Age at death: 73

Cause of death: Heart failure

Final words: Unknown

Admission to Hollywood Cemetery: Free

James Monroe's legacy is the doctrine which bears his name. Our fifth president warned Europe against intrusion in our hemisphere, a policy invoked by future administrations. Monroe, known for his genial demeanor, presided over the brief time called the "era of good feelings" for its lack of partisan divisions.

Monroe lived just six years after he left the presidency. He and his wife Elizabeth departed the White House in 1825 for Oak Hill, their newly built Virginia home. Their architect was Thomas Jefferson. Like some other presidents before him, he retired owing money; there were no pensions for presidents until the second half of the twentieth century. Monroe worked diligently to obtain back pay from the federal government, with little success. He also maintained some involvement with public

Bronze plaque marking Monroe's marble tomb

affairs, serving as president of the Virginia Constitutional Convention and as a regent at the University of Virginia. Stunned by Elizabeth's death in 1830, he was no longer able to live at Oak Hill without her. Monroe moved to New York City to live with his daughter, Maria Hester Gouverneur.

Monroe remained mentally alert into his seventies and began work on his memoirs, but his heart was weak. He developed what may have been tuberculosis during the final months of his life and died of heart failure at his daughter's home in New York City on July 4, 1831. He was the third president, following Adams and Jefferson, to die on the Fourth of July.

On July 7, city businesses closed while a public eulogy was held for Monroe at New York City Hall. Funeral services followed at St. Paul's Episcopal Church. Thousands clogged the streets as they joined a funeral procession to Marble Cemetery while a seventy-three-gun salute marked each year of Monroe's life. As mourners looked on, James Monroe's body was placed in his son-in-law's family vault.

On July 5, 1858, President Monroe's remains were moved from New York City to Hollywood Cemetery in Richmond, Virginia. The Virginia General Assembly ordered the transfer, believing that its native son should be buried on home territory. His grave now sits atop a hill in that cemetery, surrounded by a black iron cage-like monument. A bronze plaque notes that he is buried there "as an evidence of the affection of Virginia For Her Good and Honored Son." Other notable political figures are buried nearby, including President John Tyler; Jefferson Davis, president of the Confederacy; Confederate Generals Jeb Stuart and George Pickett; and U.S. Supreme Court Justice Lewis Powell.

Touring James Monroe's Tomb at Hollywood Cemetery

Hollywood Cemetery is located in Richmond, Virginia. It is open daily from 8:00 a.m. to 6:00 p.m. There is no admission fee. A tour map is sold in the office for $1.00.

From Interstate 95 southbound or Interstate 64 eastbound: Take exit 76 to Belvidere Street. Follow Belvidere south through downtown over the Downtown Expressway to Spring Street. Make a right onto Spring Street. Continue on Spring until you reach Cherry Street, and take a right onto Cherry. The entrance to the cemetery is located at the corner of Cherry and Albemarle Streets.

From Interstate 95 northbound or Interstate 64 westbound: Take exit 76/Chamberlayne Avenue and turn left off the ramp onto Chamberlayne Parkway. Follow the parkway to Leigh Street. Turn left around the Bojangles monument onto Leigh Street and follow Leigh to Belvidere Street. Turn left onto Belvidere. Follow Belvidere south through downtown over the Downtown Expressway to Spring Street. Make a right onto Spring Street. Continue on Spring until you reach Cherry Street and take a right onto Cherry. The entrance to the cemetery is located at the corner of Cherry and Albemarle Streets.

President Monroe's grave is located in President Circle. From the cemetery entrance, bear right on Hollywood Avenue. Turn left at Westvale Avenue and proceed to Hillside Avenue which leads to President Circle. Monroe is buried in the center of the circle; President John Tyler is buried on the circle's perimeter.

For additional information

Hollywood Cemetery
412 South Cherry Street
Richmond, VA 23220
Phone: (804) 648-8501
www.hollywoodcemetery.org

"As his health declined, Monroe became a near recluse...." —*Richard Norton Smith*

Monroe's final years had been demeaning. Shadowed by debt, grief-stricken over the loss of his wife, Elizabeth, the last of the Virginia Dynasty was compelled to sell his Loudoun County estate and take up residence with his daughter and son-in-law in New York City. As his health declined, Monroe became a near recluse, dosing himself with syrup of horehound for a tubercular condition. On the afternoon of July 4, 1831, he became the third American president to succumb on the nation's birthday. (Madison fell just short, dying on June 28, 1836.) Thousands turned out to watch a hearse bear his remains slowly up Broadway to a "temporary" vault, where they remained until the Virginia legislature in 1858 decided to observe the centenary of Monroe's birth with an elaborate homecoming and burial in the most bizarre of presidential tombs—a black iron birdcage-like affair that only Charles Addams could love.

— RNS

Elizabeth Monroe's grave lies next to her husband's birdcage-like tomb in Hollywood Cemetery

John Quincy Adams

Buried: United First Parish Church (Church of the Presidents), Quincy, Massachusetts

Sixth President – 1825-1829

Born: July 11, 1767, in Quincy, Massachusetts

Died: 7:20 p.m. on February 23, 1848, in Washington, D.C.

Age at death: 80

Cause of death: Stroke

Final words: "I am content" or "I am composed" (accounts vary)

Admission to United First Parish Church: $4.00

The easygoing Monroe was followed by John Quincy Adams who candidly described himself as reserved and austere. The son of our second president arrived at the White House in 1825 after a fractious election. None of the four presidential candidates captured a majority of electoral votes, so the race was decided in the House of Representatives.

Our sixth president kept in shape by walking between the White House and the Capitol. As befit his cold personality, he was also fond of skinny-dipping in the chilly waters of the Potomac. His British-born wife, Louisa, was the only first lady born outside the United States. Unhappy in her position, she avoided social occasions whenever possible.

After losing the presidency to Andrew Jackson in the election of 1828, John Quincy Adams embarked on yet another political career as the only former president to serve in the U.S. House of Representatives. In 1830, he was elected to represent a Massachusetts district. He returned to Washington and resumed his early morning swims, a habit he continued until just before his death.

Eighteen years later, at age eighty, though his health had deteriorated after a minor stroke in 1846, he was still serving in Congress. On February 21, 1848, at his desk in the House chamber, Adams suffered a second and more serious stroke. After vehemently voting to reject more decorations for some Mexican War generals, the Congressman fell into the arms of Ohio Representative David Fisher. His colleagues carried him to the Speaker's Room, just off the House floor, where he was attended by five physicians, four of whom were fellow Representatives. Accounts of Adams's last words vary. Some claimed to have heard him whisper, "I am content." Others recalled the words, "I am composed." He slipped into a coma and died at the Capitol two days later.

Adams's body lay on view in a House committee room for two days, where thousands filed past to see him. Funeral services were conducted by the House chaplain on February 25, with the coffin resting before the Speaker's rostrum in the House chamber. Adams's body was taken in a grand procession to a receiving vault at Congressional Cemetery in Washington. A few days later, it was transported back to Massachusetts by train, accompanied by a member of Congress from each state. Mourners lined the route and a public memorial service was held at Faneuil Hall in Boston. At the end of the journey, Adams was laid to rest in the family vault at the Quincy cemetery. He was eventually buried in the Adams crypt at the United First Parish Church in Quincy alongside his parents. His wife Louisa was also buried there when she died in 1852.

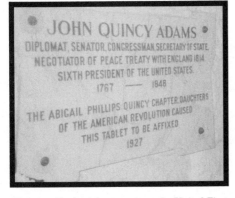

Sign outside the Adams crypt at the United First Parish Church (Church of the Presidents)

John Quincy Adams

Touring John Quincy Adams's Tomb
at United First Parish Church

United First Parish Church (Church of the Presidents) is located in Quincy, Massachusetts, about ten miles south of Boston.

From Boston: Take Interstate 93 or Route 128 south. Take exit 7, onto Route 3 South to Braintree and Cape Cod. Take the first exit off Route 3 South, marked exit 18 for Washington Street. Continue on Burgin Parkway through six traffic lights. At the seventh light, turn right onto Dimmock Street. Go one block and take a right onto Hancock Street. The church is located at 1306 Hancock Street.

The church is also accessible via the Metropolitan Boston Transit Authority's subway system. From Boston, take the red line train to the Quincy Center station. Go right when exiting the train and continue up the stairs. Take a left at the top of the stairs and exit onto Hancock Street. The church is located at 1306 Hancock Street.

The Adams family graves are located in the basement crypt. To reach the crypt after entering the church through the main doors, take a right, go down the stairs, and take a left.

Guided tours of the crypt are also available for $5.00, beginning at the Adams National Historical Park Visitors Center, located at 1250 Hancock Street. The tour also includes the John Adams birthplace and the Adams family home. Tours operate from April 19 through November 10, from 9:00 a.m. to 5:00 p.m. Admission is $5.00, free for those under sixteen.

For additional information

United First Parish Church (Church of the Presidents)
1306 Hancock Street (Quincy Center)
Quincy, MA 02169
Phone: (617) 773-0062 / Fax: (617) 773-7499
www.ufpc.org

Adams National Historical Park Visitors Center
1250 Hancock Street
Quincy, MA 02169
Phone: (617) 773-1177 / Fax: (617) 847-3015
www.nps.gov/adam/

"...the sarcophagus provided for...JQA was too small for his elaborate coffin..." —*Richard Norton Smith*

Upright and unadorned, the Quincy meetinghouse reflects the characters of the two presidents who, with their wives, share a subterranean crypt carved from solid granite. John and Abigail Adams were placed there in 1828. Twenty-four years later the area was enlarged to accommodate the remains of John Quincy and his wife Louisa. As it happened, the sarcophagus provided for the second President Adams was too small for his elaborate coffin, forcing a halt in the ceremony while stonemasons were summoned to widen the enclosure. Somehow it made perfect sense, given Adams's failure while in the White House to fit his spacious views within the cramped vision of nineteenth-century agrarianism. Almost forty years would pass before the iron grillwork fronting the Adams crypt swung open to admit the general public.

— RNS

John Quincy Adams lies next to his British-born wife Louisa in the Adams crypt

Andrew Jackson

Buried: The Hermitage, Hermitage, Tennessee

Seventh President – 1829-1837

Born: March 15, 1767, in Waxhaw, South Carolina

Died: 6:00 p.m. on June 8, 1845, at the Hermitage, Tennessee

Age at death: 78

Cause of death: Heart failure

Final words: "We shall all meet in heaven."

Admission to the Hermitage: $17.00

Andrew Jackson's reputation as a man of the people was cemented at his inauguration. After his swearing-in at the Capitol, many citizens returned with the new president to the White House. The celebration lasted throughout the night and went down in history as one of the most raucous parties ever held on the South Lawn.

Two women played prominent roles in Andrew Jackson's presidency. The first was his beloved wife, Rachel. His election campaign of 1828 was marred by charges of adultery when it became known that Rachel's divorce from her first husband was not yet final when she and Jackson married. The ensuing publicity devastated the couple. Rachel fell ill and died suddenly in December of 1828, just after the election. Andrew Jackson blamed his political enemies.

His bitterness resurfaced when Washington society snubbed the wife of his secretary of war, John Eaton, who had married Peggy Timberlake only two months after her first husband's suicide. Gossip swirled. Jackson, reminded of his late wife's anguish, stubbornly insisted that the other cabinet members and their wives treat Peggy Eaton with respect. Only Secretary of State Martin Van Buren complied. Angered over this point of honor, Jackson forced the resignation of his entire cabinet.

In March of 1837, at the end of his second, more stable term, Jackson returned alone to the Hermitage, his home near Nashville. Enormously popular, he spoke frequently on behalf of his successor, Martin Van Buren, and for a future president, James K. Polk.

Jackson was obsessed with Rachel's memory. He hung her portrait across from his bed so that it would be the first and last thing he saw each day. Over the next eight years, Jackson's health declined rapidly; tuberculosis and partial blindness rocked the strong man's body and outlook. Jackson became bloated as dropsy spread throughout his body. On June 2, 1845, a doctor operated to drain fluid from his midsection. By June 8, he had fallen unconscious. Knowing the end was near, his son Andrew and daughter-in-law Sarah gathered at his bedside. Many of the family slaves congregated outside. In his final moments, Jackson told them not to cry and hoped that they all, black and white, would meet in heaven. He died later that afternoon, at the age of seventy-eight. His friend Sam Houston, the legendary former governor of Tennessee, arrived too late to see his hero's last moments.

Andrew and Rachel Jackson are buried side-by-side under a cupola in the southeast corner of Rachel's garden. His tombstone declares him as General Andrew Jackson, not mentioning his service as President. Other members of the Jackson family, and several Jackson family slaves, are buried nearby.

Grave of Uncle Alfred, a Jackson family slave

Andrew Jackson

Touring Andrew Jackson's Tomb at the Hermitage

The Hermitage is located twelve miles east of Nashville, Tennessee.

From Nashville: Take Interstate 40 East to exit 221A (Old Hickory Boulevard). The Hermitage is located just off Old Hickory Boulevard in Hermitage, Tennessee. Signs for the Hermitage are clearly marked from the Old Hickory Boulevard exit.

Andrew Jackson's grave is visible from the main house. Look for the garden at the side of the home; Jackson's grave is located in the garden's right-hand corner, under a cupola.

The Hermitage is open from 9:30 a.m. to 5:00 p.m. April 1 through October 15 and 9:00 a.m. to 4:30 p.m. October 16 through March 31, except for Thanksgiving, Christmas, and the third week in January. Admission is $17.00 for adults, $14.00 for senior citizens, $11.00 for students ages thirteen to eighteen, and $7.00 for children ages six to twelve. Children under six are admitted free.

For additional information

The Hermitage
4580 Rachel's Lane
Hermitage, TN 37076
Phone: (615) 889-2941
Fax: (615) 889-9909
www.thehermitage.com

Andrew and Rachel Jackson lie under a stone cupola in the Hermitage garden

"Yet even as his tortured body disintegrated, his iron will remained intact." —Richard Norton Smith

That Andrew Jackson survived as long as he did is less a testimony to the vagaries of nineteenth-century medicine—the patient self-medicated himself over the years with vast dosages of lead and mercury—than to Jackson's indomitable spirit.

Somehow the old man soldiered on, notwithstanding frequent abscesses caused by two bullets lodged in his body from a youthful duel; bleeding in the lungs; malarial fever; chronic dysentery; severe toothache; malnutrition and "dropsical habits" which caused his feet and ankles to swell, and for which he took regular warm salt baths.

"Salts are injurious to all dropsical habits," Jackson told a fellow sufferer in 1813, "and calomel is the great cleanser of the blood."

By the spring of 1845, Jackson was, in his own words, "a perfect Jelly from the toes to the upper part of my abdomen, in any part of which a finger can be pressed half-an-inch and the print will remain for minutes." Due to massive edema, Jackson was literally drowning in his own fluids. Yet even as his tortured body disintegrated, his iron will remained intact. Artist G.P.A. Healy, having already completed two likenesses of the General, wished to beg off a commission to paint Jackson's beloved granddaughter Sarah because he was late for a session with Henry Clay. On learning this, the dying man's eyes blazed with indignation.

"Young man," he snapped, "always do your duty."

Healy did as he was told, leading Clay to observe, when they belatedly met, "I see that you, like all who approached that man, were fascinated."

To the end, "that man" remained faithful to his political creed. When a returning naval officer offered the former president an elaborate sarcophagus originally made for the Roman Emperor Severus, Jackson's refusal was instantaneous. "My republican feelings and principles forbid it," he wrote; "the simplicity of our system of government forbids it."

—RNS

Andrew Jackson

Martin Van Buren

Buried: Kinderhook Reformed Cemetery, Kinderhook, New York

Eighth President – 1837-1841

Born: December 5, 1782, in Kinderhook, New York

Died: 2:00 a.m. on July 24, 1862, in Kinderhook, New York

Age at death: 79

Cause of death: Heart failure

Final words: "There is but one reliance."

Admission to Kinderhook Reformed Cemetery: Free

One of the most comical and biting assessments of our eighth president, Martin Van Buren, came from Tennessee Congressman Davy Crockett. The plain-spoken frontiersman was not impressed when he encountered "what the English call a dandy." Crockett observed that "when he enters the Senate chamber in the morning, he struts and swaggers like a crow in the gutter." Crockett thought he saw corsets constricting Van Buren's ample waist and stung him further: "It would be difficult to say, from his personal appearance, whether he was man or woman." Crockett concluded that his whiskers resolved any doubt.

The dapper Van Buren was the first president born an American citizen. He served a single term before being defeated for reelection by William Henry Harrison in 1840.

Kinderhook, New York

Martin Van Buren is Kinderhook Reformed Cemetery's best-known resident

Retiring to his Lindenwald estate in Kinderhook, New York, near Albany, he plotted his comeback. Van Buren sought the presidency twice more, but was unsuccessful. Thereafter his withdrawal from public life was complete, save for an occasional editorial on current affairs. His personal time was spent gardening and visiting with lifelong friends.

In 1853 Van Buren traveled to Europe, hoping a warmer climate might help his chronic asthma. He stayed there until the summer of 1855, but his respiratory problems resurfaced when he returned. Back in New York, he also suffered a series of falls, including one in which he broke his left arm and another in which he was thrown from a horse. Van Buren's sense of humor remained intact. After the latter fall, he remarked, "Does not this not speak well of my skull?"

Van Buren was at work on his memoirs when he was stricken with pneumonia in the fall of 1861. He was bedridden thereafter. Martin Van Buren died of heart failure on Friday, July 24, 1862, at the age of seventy-nine, while at home with his sons. The announcement of his death was no surprise to the nation; rumors of the former president's ill health had been circulating for the past year.

Van Buren's funeral was held the following Monday at the Reformed Dutch Church of Kinderhook. Parishioners there remembered Van Buren for his loud singing voice—he frequently drowned out the hymns of those around him. Hundreds of mourners who could not fit into the church waited outside until it was time for the public viewing. Witnesses noted that the former president, well-dressed as always, looked quite natural in his rosewood coffin. As he had instructed, no bells were rung as Kinderhook's Fire Company No. 2 led the cortege to Kinderhook Reformed Cemetery. Martin Van Buren was laid to rest alongside his beloved wife Hannah.

Martin Van Buren

Touring Martin Van Buren's Tomb at Kinderhook Reformed Cemetery

Kinderhook Reformed Cemetery is open year-round from 9:00 a.m. until dusk. Admission is free.

From the east: Take Interstate 90 to exit B1 onto U.S. Route 9 South. At the stop light on Route 9, turn onto Albany Avenue. The cemetery is located 0.5 miles ahead on both sides of Albany Avenue.

From the west: Take Interstate 90 to exit 12 onto U.S. Route 9 South. At the stop light on Route 9, turn onto Albany Avenue. The cemetery is located 0.5 miles ahead on both sides of Albany Avenue.

Van Buren's grave is located in the northeastern section of the cemetery on the right side of Albany Avenue, the cemetery's only road.

For additional information

Columbia County
Department of Tourism
401 State Street
Hudson, NY 12534
Phone: (800) 724-1846 /
(518) 828-3375
www.columbiacountyny.org

Martin Van Buren National
Historic Site
1013 Old Post Road
Kinderhook, NY 12106
Phone: (518) 758–9689
www.nps.gov/mava

Kinderhook Reformed Chuch
23 Broad Street
Kinderhook, NY 12106
Phone: (518) 758–6401

Martin Van Buren's monument towers over the other graves in Kinderhook Reformed Cemetery

"Van Buren's final hours played out against the much greater drama of the Fraternal War…"

—Richard Norton Smith

The so-called Red Fox of Kinderhook is remembered today as a political tactician of impressive gifts and flexible principles. After defending slavery while in the White House, in 1848 he reinvented himself as the standard bearer of the Free Soil Party. A natural-born conciliator, Van Buren nevertheless rejected an appeal from Franklin Pierce that would have enlisted America's ex-presidents in calling a Peace Convention on the eve of Abraham Lincoln's first inauguration.

Van Buren's final hours played out against the much greater drama of the Fraternal War; as his life drew to its close, the man in the White House sought advice from his Cabinet about the timing of a presidential proclamation to emancipate slaves in areas still in rebellion against the United States government.

On learning of his predecessor's death, Lincoln took time out from his crushing responsibilities to draft a statement of tribute. "The grief of his patriotic friends," wrote the man in the White House, "will measurably be assuaged by the consciousness that while suffering with disease and seeing his end approaching, his prayers were for the restoration of the authority of the government of which he had been head, and for peace and good will among his fellow citizens."

Lincoln, facing hotly contested midterm elections, was not above putting words of endorsement in a dead man's mouth. The president once known as the Little Magician would have approved.

— RNS

William Henry Harrison

Buried: Harrison Tomb, North Bend, Ohio

Ninth President – 1841

Born: February 9, 1773, in Charles City County, Virginia

Died: 12:30 a.m. on April 4, 1841, at the White House, Washington, D.C.

Age at Death: 68

Cause of death: Pneumonia

Final words: "I wish you to understand the true principles of the government. I wish them carried out. I ask nothing more."

Admission to Harrison Tomb: Free

On March 4, 1841, William Henry Harrison delivered his inaugural address, which holds the record for length—over one hundred minutes. Speaking outdoors without an overcoat, Harrison vowed not to seek a second term. His promise was fulfilled, but not on his terms. Shortly after the inauguration, Harrison was caught in a downpour while out for a walk. The cold he contracted turned into pneumonia and he was soon confined to his bed. He stayed there for several days with brief signs of improvement, but Harrison seemed to sense that he was gravely ill. He reportedly remarked, "I am ill, very ill, much more so than they think." He grew delirious, but his last words reflected his awareness of his position: "I wish you to understand the true principles of the government. I wish them carried out. I ask for nothing more." On April 4 at 12:30 a.m., just one month after taking office, William Henry Harrison died quietly in his bed at the White House, the first of eight presidents to die in office.

Harrison's wife Anna had stayed behind at their home in North Bend, Ohio, to pack up their belongings. Though she planned to join her husband at the White House in May, she never made the trip.

Episcopal funeral services were conducted in the East Room of the White House, where Harrison's body was on view in an open casket. The casket was escorted up Pennsylvania Avenue from the White House by twenty-six pallbearers, one for each state. The new president, John Tyler, as well as the Cabinet, the Diplomatic Corps, and fourteen militia companies joined 10,000 mourners in the procession. Harrison's body lay in state at the Capitol before being taken to Washington's Congressional Cemetery. In June of that year, it was moved to North Bend, Ohio, where the Harrisons had made their home, for permanent burial.

Although she never lived in the White House, Anna Harrison was the first widowed presidential wife to receive a pension. President John Tyler, her husband's former neighbor in Virginia, granted her the sum of $25,000 in June of 1841. Anna Harrison was buried alongside her husband when she died in 1864.

William Henry Harrison's 100-foot funeral monument near the banks of the Ohio River

William Henry Harrison

Touring William Henry Harrison's Tomb at the Harrison Tomb State Memorial

The Harrison Tomb is located in North Bend, Ohio, fifteen miles west of Cincinnati. The tomb is open year-round during daylight hours. Admission is free.

From Cincinnati and other points east: Take U.S. Route 50 West. The Harrison Tomb is located on Cliff Road, west off U.S. Route 50. Follow the signs for the Harrison Tomb State Memorial.

From the west: Take U.S. Route 275 to Route 50 West. The Harrison Tomb is located on Cliff Road, west off Route 50. Follow the signs for the Harrison Tomb State Memorial.

Stone pillars topped by giant eagles mark the entrance to the Harrison Tomb

For additional information

Harrison Tomb
c/o Site Operations Department
The Ohio Historical Society
1982 Velma Avenue
Columbus, Ohio 43211
Phone: (800) 686-1535 /
(614) 297-2630
Fax: (614) 297-2628
www.ohiohistory.org/
places/harrison

"...Harrison, no master of the sound bite, is the only American president to die from talking too much."

—Richard Norton Smith

Ohio boasts chief executives whose chief claim to modern recollection is their funerary monuments. For instance, it took longer to build William Henry Harrison's hundred-foot shaft overlooking the Ohio River at North Bend, dedicated in 1924, than it did for Harrison to seek, win, and fill the presidency. Contracting pneumonia after delivering a lengthy inaugural address in March 1841, the sixty-eight-year-old Harrison, no master of the sound bite, is the only American president to die from talking too much.

At the Hermitage, his estate outside Nashville, Andrew Jackson could hardly contain his delight at the news. "A kind and overruling providence has interfered to prolong our glorious Union and happy republican system," Jackson told his old henchman, Francis P. Blair, "which General Harrison and his Cabinet were preparing to destroy under the dictation of the profligate demagogue, Henry Clay." Fortunately, Harrison's death put a halt to such dire possibilities. "The Lord ruleth, let our nation rejoice," Jackson added with a flourish, in a display of partisan bad taste unparalleled in American history.

— RNS

John Tyler

Buried: Hollywood Cemetery, Richmond, Virginia

Tenth President – 1841-1845

Born: March 29, 1790, in Charles City County, Virginia

Died: 12:15 a.m. on January 18, 1862, in Richmond, Virginia

Age at death: 71

Cause of death: Bilious fever

Final words: "Perhaps it is best."

Admission to Hollywood Cemetery: Free

Willam Henry Harrison's swift and untimely death in 1841 elevated John Tyler to the presidency and earned him the nickname "His Accidency." At his home in Virginia only a month after the inauguration and unaware of Harrison's illness, Tyler was shocked to learn of his ascendance to the nation's highest office.

In 1845, after nearly four fractious years as president, Tyler returned to Sherwood Forest, his plantation near Richmond. Remarried after the death of his first wife to a woman thirty years his junior, Tyler fathered seven additional children after leaving the White House. Our most prolific president, he had fourteen children who lived to maturity.

He remained deeply involved in politics and as the Civil War drew near, supported secession for his beloved Virginia. In

WILLIAM
HENRY
HARRISON.
SECRETARY OF THE
NORTHWEST TERRITORY.
DELEGATE OF THE NORTHWEST
TERRITORY TO CONGRESS.
TERRITORIAL GOVERNOR
OF INDIANA.
MEMBER OF CONGRESS FROM
OHIO.
OHIO STATE SENATOR.
UNITED STATES SENATOR
FROM OHIO.
MINISTER TO COLOMBIA.
NINTH PRESIDENT OF
THE UNITED STATES.

ABOVE: The stepping stones of William Henry Harrison's political career are etched in these columns marking his gravesite in North Bend, Ohio, fifteen miles west of Cincinnati.

PREVIOUS PAGE: Martin Van Buren rests in Kinderhook Cemetery, twenty miles south of Albany, New York.

JOHN TYLER
PRESIDENT
OF THE
UNITED STATES
1841 1845
BORN
IN CHARLES CITY COUNTY VA
MARCH 29 1790
DIED
IN THE CITY OF RICHMOND
JANUARY 18 1862

John Tyler lies within yards of James Monroe, another Virginia president, in Richmond's Hollywood Cemetery.

The Tennessee State Capitol in Nashville provides the backdrop for James K. Polk's final resting place.

Zachary Taylor, known as "Old Rough and Ready" for his rumpled appearance in battle, is buried in a national cemetery named for him in Louisville, Kentucky.

ABOVE: Each year on January 7, a crowd gathers at Millard Fillmore's grave in Buffalo, New York to mark the former president's birthday.

OPPOSITE: Branded a traitor for his support of the Confederacy, Franklin Pierce was not recognized with a monument until 1946, when the state of New Hampshire erected a granite memorial at his gravesite in Concord's Old North Cemetery.

JANE M. APPLETON
WIFE OF
FRANKLIN PIERCE
BORN MAR. 12, 1806
DIED DEC. 2, 1863

FRANKLIN PIERCE
BORN NOV. 23, 1804
DIED OCT. 8, 1869

14 TH PRESIDENT
OF THE
UNITED STATES
1853 ——— 1857

THEIR CHILDREN
FRANK R. PIERCE
BORN AUG. 27, 1839
DIED NOV. 14, 1843
BENJAMIN PIERCE
BORN APR. 13, 1841
DIED JAN. 6, 1853

PIERCE

James Buchanan selected his own burial spot in Lancaster, Pennsylvania's Woodward Hill Cemetery.

November of 1861 he was again elected to public office as a member of the Confederate House of Representatives.

Tyler did not live to serve the Confederacy. He arrived in Richmond, the Confederate capital, to begin his term, and moved into the Exchange Hotel. His wife Julia met him there on January 10, 1862. Though she had not planned to join him so soon, she grew alarmed after dreaming that her husband was gravely ill. Two days after her arrival, Tyler became sick and collapsed in the hotel dining room. His physician determined that Tyler was suffering from bronchitis and liver dysfunction, then known as "bilious fever." The doctor prescribed morphine and ordered the former president to bed. The Tylers planned to return to Sherwood Forest, but the night before their departure, John Tyler took a turn for the worse. He awoke with difficulty breathing in the middle of the night. A doctor arrived, but there was nothing to be done. Moments before he died, Tyler said, "Perhaps it is best."

John Tyler's grave stands near James Monroe's tomb in Richmond's Hollywood Cemetery

John Tyler's body lay in state at the Confederate Congress in Richmond with a Confederate flag covering the open casket. Following the funeral at St. Paul's Episcopal Church, a procession of over 150 carriages followed Tyler's coffin to Richmond's Hollywood Cemetery. He was buried near another former president, James Monroe. Because his active support for the Confederacy was unpopular with officials in Washington, Tyler's death was virtually ignored by the federal government. This president was viewed as a Confederate and buried near its government. Congress did not place an official marker at his gravesite until more than fifty years later.

John Tyler

Touring John Tyler's Tomb at Hollywood Cemetery

Hollywood Cemetery is located in Richmond, Virginia. It is open daily from 8:00 a.m. to 6:00 p.m. There is no admission fee. A tour map is sold in the office for $1.00.

From Interstate 95 southbound or Interstate 64 eastbound: Take exit 76 to Belvidere Street. Follow Belvidere south through downtown over the Downtown Expressway to Spring Street. Make a right onto Spring Street. Continue on Spring until you reach Cherry Street and take a right onto Cherry. The entrance to the cemetery is located at the corner of Cherry and Albemarle Streets.

From Interstate 95 northbound or Interstate 64 westbound: Take exit 76/Chamberlayne Avenue and turn left off the ramp onto Chamberlayne Parkway. Follow the parkway to Leigh Street. Turn left around the Bojangles monument onto Leigh Street and follow Leigh to Belvidere Street. Turn left onto Belvidere. Follow Belvidere south through downtown over the Downtown Expressway to Spring Street. Make a right onto Spring Street. Continue on Spring until you reach Cherry Street and take a right onto Cherry. The entrance to the cemetery is located at the corner of Cherry and Albemarle Streets.

President Tyler's grave is located in President Circle. From the cemetery entrance, bear right on Hollywood Avenue. Turn left at Westvale Avenue and proceed to Hillside Avenue which leads to President Circle. James Monroe is buried in the center of the circle; Tyler is buried on the circle's perimeter.

For additional information

Hollywood Cemetery
412 South Cherry Street
Richmond, VA 23220
Phone: (804) 648-8501
www.hollywoodcemetery.org

"…John Tyler, died a traitor." —*Richard Norton Smith*

To date, no American president has been cremated, although many have been condemned to the flames of academic purgatory. One member of the fraternity, John Tyler, died a traitor. After failing to secure a peaceful settlement of sectional differences in the winter of 1860-61, Tyler, a native Virginian, followed his state into the Confederacy. His passing in January 1862, came before he took his seat in the Confederate Congress. Jefferson Davis and other high rebel officials accompanied his cortege to Richmond's Hollywood Cemetery where Davis himself would rest one day, part of a presidential trifecta that includes James Monroe, a Virginian of stauncher nationalist sympathies.

— RNS

James K. Polk

Buried: State Capitol, Nashville, Tennessee

Eleventh President – 1845-1849

Born: November 2, 1795, in Mecklenburg County, North Carolina

Died: June 15, 1849, in Nashville, Tennessee

Age at death: 53

Cause of death: Undetermined, possibly cholera

Final words: "I love you, Sarah, for all eternity, I love you."

Admission to State Capitol: Free

Despite being one of the younger presidents, Democrat James Polk was eager to fulfill his promise to retire at the end of his first term. A workaholic, he spent much of his presidency consumed by the war with Mexico. He wrote in his diary of the prospect, "I am sure I shall be a happier man in my retirement than I have been during the four years I have filled the highest office in the gift of my countrymen."

Polk purchased a Nashville home, which he dubbed Polk Place and set about organizing his political papers and remodeling the home to his tastes. He had been retired from the presidency for only three months when he went on a tour of the southern states. He made the mistake of stopping in New Orleans, where a cholera epidemic had recently broken out. Polk became sick shortly thereafter. He quickly grew weaker and died on June 15, 1849, at the age of fifty-three. The prevailing feeling at the time was that the arduous duties of the presidency may have weakened Polk's constitution, leaving him vulnerable to infection and unable to fight off the disease.

James Polk was immediately buried in a common cemetery with thirty-two other victims of the cholera epidemic. Local officials believed that the quick disposal of bodies would prevent spread of the disease. Polk was later given the honors accorded a former president and was laid to rest at Polk Place.

Polk's wife Sarah lived at Polk Place for forty-two more years. A proper Victorian widow, she wore black the entire time. When she died in 1891, she was buried alongside him. Despite Polk's specific instructions that their home should be given to the state of Tennessee, Polk Place was demolished after Sarah's death. The bodies of James and Sarah Polk were moved to the grounds of the Tennessee State Capitol in Nashville in 1893.

Polk's third and final resting place

Touring James K. Polk's Tomb at the Tennessee State Capitol

James K. Polk's grave is located on the grounds of the state capitol building in downtown Nashville, Tennessee. The capitol is open 9:00 a.m. until 4:00 p.m., Monday through Friday. The grounds are also open on weekends. Limited street parking is available in the area. There is no admission fee.

From I-40: Exit on Broadway (exit 209A from I-40W; exit 209B from I-40E), going toward downtown. Turn left on Fifth Avenue and go three blocks. The museum is on the left between Union and Deaderick Streets.

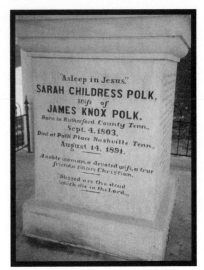

Sarah Polk, who lived forty-two years after her husband's death, was buried beside him in 1891. The bodies of James and Sarah Polk were moved to the state capitol grounds two years later.

For additional information

Tennessee State Capitol
Charlotte Avenue and 7th Avenue, North
Nashville, TN 37243
Phone: (615) 741-2692
www.tnmuseum.org

"On his deathbed, Polk sought baptism into the Methodist Church..." —*Richard Norton Smith*

For many men, retirement provides a whole new lease on life. In Polk's case, it was a very short lease indeed. Never blessed with robust health, in the spring of 1849, the former president came down with a debilitating illness. "My bowels were affected and the shaking of the Boat had become inconvenient to me," he acknowledged outside Memphis, where one doctor ruled out cholera. In fact, some believe Polk was afflicted with chronic diarrhea, a frequent complaint in the unsanitary nineteenth century. On his deathbed, Polk sought baptism into the Methodist Church—thus defying his mother, who had arrived, minister in tow, in hope of making her dying son a Presbyterian.

A personal note: As it happens, my Harvard roommate is a Polk descendant. I won't lower the intellectual or other standards of the present volume by quoting our ribald exchanges concerning the final hours of his distinguished ancestor; suffice it to say I learned as a sophomore where sophomoric humor gets its name.

— RNS

Polk's grave on the grounds of the Tennessee State Capitol

James K. Polk

Zachary Taylor

Buried: Zachary Taylor National Cemetery, Louisville, Kentucky

Twelfth President – 1849-1850

Born: November 24, 1784, in Orange County, Virginia

Died: 10:35 p.m. on July 9, 1850, in Washington, D.C.

Age at death: 65

Cause of death: Cholera

Final words: "I am sorry that I am about to leave my friends."

Admission to Zachary Taylor National Cemetery: Free

The hero of the Mexican War known as "Old Rough and Ready," Zachary Taylor was the first president to die in office while Congress was in session. He had served a little over a year, much of it consumed by sectional issues. Though a slaveholder himself, Taylor opposed secession and the extension of slavery into new territories. He did not live to see the conflict resolved. On the Fourth of July, 1850, Taylor attended groundbreaking ceremonies for the Washington Monument in sweltering heat. Upon returning to the White House, he devoured a large bowl of fruit and some cold milk. He became severely ill later that day. A doctor diagnosed cholera, an inflammation of the stomach and intestines, the result of having eaten food that had not been properly refrigerated. The president was given drugs and improved

Gary Peak, former director of the Zachary Taylor National Cemetery, points to list of Mexican War battles in which "Old Rough and Ready" fought. This final granite marker to Taylor has a misspelling. The last entry should read Buena Vista.

slightly. By July 8, however, his condition worsened. Doctors blistered his skin and bled his veins in the hope of freeing his body from infection. Taylor himself sensed their efforts were futile. That evening he reportedly said, "I am about to die. I expect the summons very soon. I have tried to discharge my duties faithfully. I regret nothing, but I am sorry that I am about to leave my friends." He died at 10:35 p.m. in his bed at the White House. His wife Peggy became hysterical and forbid the embalming of his body. She also prevented the molding of a death mask, but finally permitted an artist to draw the president in death.

The ceremonies honoring the president were extensive. Taylor's body lay in state for public viewing in the East Room of the White House until funeral services were held there on July 13. More than one hundred carriages joined the funeral procession as his body was taken to Congressional Cemetery in Washington. His favorite horse, "Old Whitey,"

accompanied the cortege. Henry Clay and Daniel Webster were among
the pallbearers. In October of that year, his remains were moved to
a family cemetery, now the Zachary Taylor National Cemetery in
Louisville, Kentucky.

Touring the Tomb at Zachary Taylor National Cemetery

Zachary Taylor National Cemetery is located in Louisville, Kentucky.
The cemetery office is open Monday through Friday from 8:00 a.m.
to 4:30 p.m., but the gates to the cemetery are open sunrise to sunset.
Admission is free.

To reach the cemetery: Take U.S. Route 64 to Route 264 East. From
Route 264, take the Route 42/Brownsboro Road exit. At the exit, take a
left onto U.S. Route 42 West/Brownsboro Road and follow the signs to
Zachary Taylor National Cemetery.

The cemetery contains only one main road which leads directly
from the cemetery entrance to Taylor's gravesite.

For additional information

Zachary Taylor National Cemetery
4701 Brownsboro Road
Louisville, KY 40207
Phone: (502) 893-3852
www.cem.va.gov/cems/nchp/ZacharyTaylor.asp

"For a few days the country's twelfth president was back in the headlines..." —*Richard Norton Smith*

For Zachary Taylor, eternal rest was anything but. It was bad enough that "Old Rough and Ready" suffered an agonizing death from cholera in July 1850. Margaret Taylor had her husband's casket opened three times before interment in order that she might gaze upon his lifeless features. The pattern repeated itself 141 years later, when a prospective academic biographer, persuaded that Taylor may have been poisoned by his political enemies, obtained permission to remove the general's mortal remains from the mausoleum in which they had rested just outside Louisville, Kentucky since early in this century. Oliver Stone, it appeared, had no monopoly on conspiracy theories. For a few days the country's twelfth president was back in the headlines, a perfect USA Today story, lacking only a front page poll and graphic of Taylor astride "Old Whitey," his Mexican War mount. All glory is fleeting, however: when tests for arsenic proved negative, Taylor returned to Louisville and the obscurity that has enshrouded him since death.

— RNS

Zachary Taylor National Cemetery is the final resting place for hundreds of military veterans

Zachary Taylor

Millard Fillmore

Buried: Forest Lawn Cemetery, Buffalo, New York

Thirteenth President – 1850-1853

Born: January 7, 1800, in Cayuga County, New York

Died: 11:10 p.m. on March 8, 1874, in Buffalo, New York

Age at death: 74

Cause of death: Stroke

Final words: "The nourishment is palatable."

Admission to Forest Lawn Cemetery: Free

Best known for being one of the least known presidents, Millard Fillmore was the last Whig to win the White House. The most notable achievement of his administration was the Compromise of 1850, which delayed civil war over the slavery issue. On a more personal level, the book-loving Fillmore and wife Abigail (his former school teacher) wrangled Congressional funds to establish a White House library. The two amassed the home's first permanent collection during Fillmore's single term as president.

Sadly, Abigail caught a cold at the inauguration of her husband's successor, Franklin Pierce, and died several weeks later. Millard Fillmore soon remarried and traveled widely in Europe with his second wife Caroline, with the hope that a milder climate would benefit her chronic health problems.

Sign marking Millard Fillmore's grave

He retained an interest in public affairs, and was even nominated to the presidency again in 1856 by the American—or Know-Nothing—Party, but was unsuccessful. He remained in good health into his later years, saying, "My health is perfect. I eat, drink and sleep as well as ever, and take a deep but silent interest in public affairs, and if Mrs. Fillmore's health can be restored, I should feel that I was in the enjoyment of an earthly paradise."

While trying to shave on the morning of February 13, 1874, the seventy-four-year-old Fillmore lost all sensation in the left side of his body. He had just suffered his first stroke. He regained partial use of his left side until he was stricken with a second stroke later that month. This time his throat muscles were severely affected, limiting his ability to swallow. Shortly before his death, in response to a doctor's question about the food he was given, Fillmore responded with his last words, "The nourishment is palatable." On March 8, Fillmore fell unconscious and died. At the announcement of his death, President Ulysses S. Grant issued a proclamation honoring the former president and flags in Fillmore's hometown of Buffalo were lowered to half mast.

Millard Fillmore's funeral was held the following Thursday, March 12. His body was kept in a rosewood coffin in the west room of the family home on Niagara Square, where a private service was held for family and close friends. At his head was a crown of camellias and rosebuds; a wreath and two large crosses lay on the coffin's lid. After the private service, Fillmore's body was borne into the hearse by Company D of the Buffalo City Guards. The cortege then traveled to St. Paul's Cathedral where the body lay in state in the vestibule for viewing by thousands of mourners. Delegations from the U.S. Senate and House of Representatives came to pay their respects, as did Buffalo's mayor. The *New York Times* reported, "Although much emaciated, Mr. Fillmore's face bore the courtly appearance so characteristic of him in life."

Following a brief and solemn service, the City Guards, the National Guard, and the U.S. Infantry led the flag-covered hearse and a long line of carriages to Fillmore's final resting place. Local businesses were closed and the procession route was lined with mourners. Prior to his death, Millard Fillmore had chosen his burial site at Forest Lawn Cemetery in Buffalo. Also buried at the site are his two wives, Abigail and Caroline, both of his children, and the mother of his first wife.

Touring Millard Fillmore's Tomb at Forest Lawn Cemetery

Forest Lawn Cemetery is located in Buffalo, New York. The cemetery is open daily from 8:00 a.m. to 7:00 p.m. from April through October and from 8:00 a.m. to 6:00 p.m. the rest of the year. Admission is free.

To reach the cemetery from the north: From Route 190 South, take exit N-11 to Route 198 East. Take the Delaware Avenue exit, and turn right on to Delaware Avenue. Turn left into the cemetery gates at the corner of Delavan Avenue and Delaware Avenue.

From the south: Take I-190 North. Take the Church Street exit and turn right onto Church Street. Take a left onto Route 384. Continue on Route 384 through the roundabout. Turn right onto Delaware Avenue.

The cemetery is located at 1411 Delaware Avenue. After entering through the gates near the administration building, follow the paths heading north (parallel to Delaware Avenue) to the cemetery's section F. On the right is a sign directing you to Millard Fillmore's grave in section F.

Fillmore's tall obelisk is surrounded by the graves of his two wives, children, and mother-in-law

For additional information

Forest Lawn Cemetery
1411 Delaware Avenue
Buffalo, NY 14209
Phone: (716) 885-1600
Fax: (716) 881-6482
www.forest-lawn.com

"...Fillmore had himself become something of a historic site." —*Richard Norton Smith*

Gateway to Forest Lawn Cemetery, the thirteenth president's chosen resting place

In his declining years, Fillmore busied himself with numerous civic organizations benefiting his cherished Buffalo. None held more appeal for him than the Buffalo Historical Society, which was only appropriate since, by then, Fillmore had himself become something of a historic site. With true Chamber of Commerce gusto, he predicted, "Buffalo...is destined by its position to be what Alexandria and Venice were."

Any man who could see Babylon in nineteenth-century Buffalo was a natural born optimist and therefore a soft touch for every sort of worthy cause involving the solicitation of funds. Having chaired a campaign to erect a suitable Soldiers and Sailors Monument, a commemorative task uncompleted at the time of his death, Fillmore would not have been surprised to learn how many years it would take before the people of Buffalo placed his own statue before their City Hall on Niagara Square. But it is not the magnet that attracts the attention of Fillmore cultists today. That honor belongs to the pink granite obelisk at Forest Lawn Cemetery where, each year, a small crowd gathers to mark Fillmore's birthday and to mock his obscure place in presidential annals.

— RNS

Franklin Pierce

Buried: Old North Cemetery, Concord, New Hampshire

Fourteenth President – 1853-1857

Born: November 23, 1804, in Hillsboro, New Hampshire

Died: 4:40 a.m. on October 8, 1869, in Concord, New Hampshire

Age at death: 64

Cause of death: Stomach inflammation

Final words: Unknown

Admission to Old North Cemetery: Free

Franklin Pierce was the only presidential candidate to have his campaign biography penned by a literary immortal, in this case Nathaniel Hawthorne. Both native New Englanders, the two men were college classmates and lifelong friends.

Labeled by many historians as one of our less successful presidents, Franklin Pierce lost the nomination for a second term to James Buchanan in 1856. He was among the first presidents to enjoy financial stability after leaving the White House. Nonetheless, his twelve-year retirement was not a happy one. Since the eve of Pierce's inauguration, when their son Bennie was killed in a train accident, both Pierce and his wife Jane battled depression. Already prone to heavy drinking, Pierce's problem grew worse after returning home to Concord, New Hampshire. Hoping to stave off melancholy,

Franklin and Jane Pierce spent some time in Europe and the Bahamas, but with little improvement.

Upon his return to Concord in 1860, Pierce spoke sympathetically of the Confederacy. Although he stopped shy of supporting secession, he was branded a traitor and was ostracized for the rest of his life. When Jane died of tuberculosis in 1863, the former president was truly alone.

By the summer of 1869, Pierce was suffering from dropsy, an accumulation of fluids in his body. He died of the disease at 4:40 a.m. on October 8, 1869, at the age of sixty-four. News of his poor health had been telegraphed frequently across the country, so his death came as no surprise.

Pierce's gravestone

Despite his unpopularity in his home state, Franklin Pierce was given the standard honors for a former president. For three days, his body, resting in a coffin covered in black cloth, lay in state with a large floral cross suspended overhead in Doric Hall at the New Hampshire State Capitol.

On October 11 twelve pallbearers, all fellow members of the state bar, carried the casket to St. Paul's Episcopal Church in Concord. A procession of local citizens and public school students followed the cortege. At the mayor's request, all local businesses closed for the duration of the funeral service. On order from President Grant, public buildings in Washington were draped in mourning. Flags were lowered to half mast in cities across the country, and the Brooklyn Navy Yard fired a thirty-one-gun salute in Pierce's honor.

Dr. John Splaine, C-SPAN's consulting historian, points to the historic marker at the Old North Cemetery

Franklin Pierce

He was buried in Concord's Old North Cemetery alongside his wife and their three children. In 1914, after much debate, the state of New Hampshire erected a bronze statue of Pierce on the capitol grounds and in 1946 finally placed a granite memorial at his grave.

Touring Franklin Pierce's Tomb at the Old North Cemetery

The Old North Cemetery is located in Concord, New Hampshire.

From Concord State Capitol: From the capitol, drive north on Main Street to Park Street. Turn left onto Park Street. Drive 0.2 miles to State Street. Continue on State Street for another 0.7 miles until you reach Old North Cemetery. Parking is available on State Street. Inside the Old North Cemetery, walk straight ahead for approximately seventy-five feet. From that point, walk ten feet to the right to President Pierce's grave. The Old North Cemetery is open every day during daylight hours. Admission is free.

Franklin Pierce outlived his wife and three children. They are buried with him in the Old North Cemetery.

For Additional Information

New Hampshire
Historical Society
30 Park Street
Concord, NH 03301
Phone: (603) 856-0641
www.nhhistory.org

City of Concord
41 Green Street
Concord, NH 03301
Phone: (603) 225-8570
www.onconcord.com

"...there is undoubtedly a tragic quality to America's fourteenth president." —*Richard Norton Smith*

*T*hough hardly a figure of Shakespearian dimensions, there is undoubtedly a tragic quality to America's fourteenth president. The youngest ever to hold that office when he was sworn in 1853, whatever chance he had for success was crushed, along with his eleven-year-old son, Bennie, killed a few weeks earlier in a horrible train wreck as his parents looked on. For Bennie's mother, Jane, a strict Calvinist who blamed her husband's political ambitions for the loss of their child, the White House was a well-furnished purgatory. Her death in December 1863, wounded Pierce's spirit, while the passing of his dearest friend, Nathaniel Hawthorne, the following spring, dramatized the political ostracism caused by Pierce's pro-southern record in office. At Hawthorne's funeral the former president was excluded from the ranks of pallbearers, which included the likes of Emerson, Longfellow, and Whittier. Instead, Pierce remained behind the other mourners in Sleepy Hollow Cemetery, to scatter a few blossoms into the open grave.

When his own casket was borne into Saint Paul's in October 1869, the ceremonies were formalistic, the grief contained. Concord's farewell to its "Man Who Might Have Been" recalled nothing so much as Longfellow's lyric written for Hawthorne's obsequies.

"How beautiful it was,
    that one bright day
In the long week of rain!
Though all its splendor could
    not chase away
The omnipresent pain."

— RNS

James Buchanan

Buried: Woodward Hill Cemetery, Lancaster, Pennsylvania

Fifteenth President — 1857-1861

Born: April 23, 1791, in Cove Gap, Pennsylvania

Died: 8:30 a.m. on June 1, 1868, in Lancaster, Pennsylvania

Age at death: 77

Cause of death: Pneumonia

Final words: "Oh Lord, God Almighty, as Thou wilt."

Admission to Woodward Hill Cemetery: Free

James Buchanan is known as our only bachelor president. Less familiar is the story of Buchanan's early romance with a young woman named Anne Coleman. She died suddenly in 1819, shortly after they had quarreled. Buchanan suffered when rumors of suicide circulated, along with claims that he was only interested in her money. He declared that his happiness would be "buried with her in the grave" and that the cause of their breakup would be revealed in a letter released after his death.

It's said that Buchanan first ran for Congress in 1820 to escape his grief and the gossip mills in his hometown of Lancaster, Pennsylvania. However, rumormongering has followed him into the modern age. Buchanan's choice of a

Washington roommate—
flamboyant fellow senator
William Rufus DeVane King—
has led to speculation about his
personal life. Lacking a wife to
handle White House social
duties, Buchanan asked his
niece, Harriet Lane, to serve as
his first lady when he won the
presidency in 1856.

The inscription on Buchanan's grave

Weary of the slavery issue, he
declined to seek a second term and left the White House for his
Wheatland estate, where he received a hero's welcome and settled into
a quiet retirement. He lived just seven more years. In his final days,
Buchanan suffered from rheumatism and dysentery. These maladies left
him susceptible to infection. In May of 1868, Buchanan contracted
pneumonia. Sensing that the end was near, he did not leave his bedroom.
James Buchanan died alone on June 1, 1868, at the age of seventy-seven.

The city of Lancaster held a public meeting in his honor. His body
lay on view in the main hall at Wheatland. Mourners and curiosity
seekers found the former president dressed in his typical white tie and
high collar shirt. A two-and-a-half mile funeral parade followed, with
bands, 125 carriages, and thousands of onlookers.

Two days before his death
Buchanan gave final instructions to
Hiram Swarr, the executor of his
estate. First, he wanted a simple obelisk
for his tomb. Second, the letter
explaining his broken engagement was
to be burned, unopened. Both orders
were obeyed. He was buried at
Woodward Hill Cemetery in Lancaster,
where a white marble monument
stands today.

*Historic marker at Woodward Hill
Cemetery*

James Buchanan

Touring James Buchanan's Tomb at Woodward Hill Cemetery

Woodward Hill Cemetery is located in Lancaster, Pennsylvania. It is open daily during the daylight hours. Admission is free.

From Philadelphia: Take the Pennsylvania Turnpike (I-76) West to exit 21. Drive south on Highway 222. Highway 222 turns into Prince Street. From Prince Street turn left onto Hager Street. On reaching Queen Street turn right.

From Harrisburg: Take Highway 283 east to the Harrisburg Pike exit. Take Harrisburg Pike west into the city of Lancaster. Harrisburg Pike turns into Harrisburg Avenue. Turn left onto Prince Street until reaching Hager Street; then turn left onto Queen Street.

To find Buchanan's grave, bear to the right after entering the cemetery gates. Climb up the small hill and head toward the red brick church. President Buchanan's gravesite is located to the left of the church.

Also buried at Woodward Hill is Frederick Muhlenberg, Speaker of the U.S. House of Representatives, 1789–1791 and 1793–1795.

For additional information

Woodward Hill Cemetery
South Queen Street
Lancaster, PA 17602

Lancaster County Historical Society
230 North President Avenue
Lancaster, PA 17603
Phone: (717) 392-4633
www.lancasterhistory.org

"Buchanan proved no more successful as a prophet than a president." —*Richard Norton Smith*

Before going to work as a screenwriter for the Weinstein brothers, Shakespeare observed that, "the evil that men do lives after them. The good is oft interred with their bones." The sentiment applies with unmistakable force to James Buchanan, the sine qua non of executive enfeeblement. The swashbuckling Theodore Roosevelt liked nothing better than to contrast "Buchanan presidents" and "Lincoln presidents," leaving no doubt as to in which camp he belonged.

Reproached for his conduct on the eve of Fort Sumter, Buchanan in retirement wrote a self-serving memoir, selected a burial spot in Lancaster's Woodward Hills Cemetery, and composed an inscription for his white marble tombstone. "I have no regret for any public act of my life, and history will vindicate my memory," he told those gathered around his sickbed in June 1868. Buchanan proved no more successful as a prophet than a president.

— *RNS*

James Buchanan's gravesite

James Buchanan

Abraham Lincoln

Buried: Oak Ridge Cemetery, Springfield, Illinois

Sixteenth President – 1861-1865

Born: February 12, 1809, in Hardin County, Kentucky

Died: 7:22 a.m. on April 15, 1865, in Washington, D.C.

Age at death: 56

Cause of death: Gunshot wound to the head

Final words: Unknown

Admission to Oak Ridge Cemetery: Free

In his 1858 bid for an Illinois Senate seat, Abraham Lincoln engaged in a series of seven debates with incumbent Democrat Stephen Douglas. The frontier lawyer lost that election, but the fame he gained allowed him to face Douglas again in the 1860 presidential race. Lincoln won the White House, inheriting a nation bitterly divided over the slavery issue.

The Civil War began just one month into Lincoln's first term and became the defining event of his administration. Sectional differences cast the industrial North against those in the South who favored states' rights. Eleven southern states seceded from the Union and formed their own Confederate government, laying the groundwork for the bloody clash that began in April 1861. Lincoln was determined to save the Union above all else.

Lincoln's final resting place at Oak Ridge Cemetery

Lincoln's 1862 Emancipation Proclamation granted freedom to slaves in the seceding states. Despite considerable losses on the battlefields, the war continued to rage for three more years. The conflict officially ended with the surrender of the Confederacy on April 9, 1865, shortly after Lincoln's second inauguration.

For many, the hostilities lived on. Unable to accept the South's defeat, an actor named John Wilkes Booth plotted against the Union government, conspiring to kidnap President Abraham Lincoln, Vice President Andrew Johnson, and Secretary of State William Seward. The scheme took a more violent turn when Booth decided that Lincoln must die. He went to Ford's Theatre in Washington on Good Friday, April 14, 1865, where Lincoln and his wife Mary Todd were attending a performance of the comedy *Our American Cousin.* Booth entered the presidential box when the policeman on guard stepped away from his post. Approaching from behind, he shot Lincoln once in the back of the head. Laughter and applause from the audience nearly drowned out the sound of the fatal gunshot. Booth jumped over the balcony and landed on the stage, where he yelled *"Sic semper tyrannis!"* before running out of the theater. A distraught Mary Todd Lincoln cried out, "They have shot the President!" as a doctor raced to the mortally injured man.

Abraham Lincoln

The president was taken to a boarding house across the street from the theater, but never regained consciousness. He died on April 15, 1865, at 7:22 a.m., the first American president to die at the hands of an assassin. A grief-stricken Secretary of War Edwin Stanton pronounced him dead with the famous line, "Now he belongs to the ages."

A funeral carriage brought Lincoln's body back to the White House. Doctors performed an autopsy and undertakers prepared his body for burial. Lincoln was dressed in the same black suit he had worn just weeks before for his second inaugural.

Funeral arrangements were extensive. The White House was heavily draped in black and church bells tolled throughout the city. Government offices and businesses closed. Lincoln's body lay in state first at the Capitol rotunda in Washington, then in cities across the country. Inconsolable, Mary Todd Lincoln refused to join in the national funeral services.

Hundreds of thousands of Americans lined the 1700-mile route as a train carried Lincoln's body back home to Springfield, Illinois. The "Lincoln Special," as it was known, retraced the path the president traveled on his way to the White House in 1861. Its stops included Baltimore, Philadelphia, New York, and Chicago. When Lincoln's body arrived in Springfield after two weeks on display, his discolored features so distressed spectators that an undertaker was called in to conceal the decay.

After a public viewing at the Illinois State Capitol, the martyred president's remains were taken for burial at Oak Ridge Cemetery. His mahogany coffin was interred together with that of his beloved son Willie, who had died in the White House at the age of eleven. Mary Todd Lincoln was buried with them in the family tomb when she died in 1882.

John Wilkes Booth was captured twelve days after the assassination and died as a result of the struggle. Historians are uncertain whether he was wounded by his pursuers or by his own hand. Four of his co-conspirators were found guilty and hanged for their roles in the scheme.

Touring Abraham Lincoln's Tomb at Oak Ridge Cemetery

The Lincoln Tomb State Historic Site is located at Oak Ridge Cemetery in Springfield, Illinois. It is open Labor Day through February, 9:00 a.m. to 4:00 p.m. (closed Sunday and Monday), and March through October, 9:00 a.m. to 5:00 p.m. daily. It is closed on major holidays. Admission is free.

From the South: Take I-55 North to the Sixth Street exit. Follow Sixth Street through downtown Springfield. Take a left onto North Grand Avenue. From North Grand Avenue, take a right onto Monument Avenue to reach Oak Ridge Cemetery.

From the North: Take I-55 South to the Sherman exit. From the exit, follow Business Route 55 (Veterans Parkway). Take a left onto J David Jones Parkway. Go approximately one mile, then take a left into Oak Ridge Cemetery.

Lincoln's tomb is clearly visible from the cemetery's main road.

The receiving vault where Lincoln's body was first held

For additional information

Site Manager
Lincoln Tomb State Historic Site
Oak Ridge Cemetery
1500 Monument Avenue
Springfield, IL 62702
Phone: (217) 782-2717
www.illinoishistory.gov

"Over the next quarter century, Springfield's city fathers buried and reburied their most famous citizen." —*Richard Norton Smith*

The most revered of presidents has suffered posthumous indignities that Jeb Stuart wouldn't wish on his worst Yankee enemy. To begin with, there was Lincoln's funeral, which at twenty days was prolonged even by the lugubrious standards of the day. Too prostrate with grief to accompany her husband's remains to Illinois, Mary Lincoln found solace by quarreling with her Springfield neighbors, whose plan to entomb Lincoln in a downtown city lot she loudly vetoed. She insisted that Lincoln be interred in rural Oak Ridge Cemetery, a parklike setting modeled after such recently consecrated beauty spots as Boston's Mount Auburn and Brooklyn's Greenwood.

Alternatively, Mrs. Lincoln would consign her husband to the basement crypt in the Capitol that had originally been reserved for George Washington.

In defense of the much maligned widow, there is something about a funeral that brings out the worst in people—within hours of John F. Kennedy's assassination, an Iowa congressman and self-proclaimed watchdog of the treasury named H.R. Gross questioned the cost of placing an eternal flame over Arlington's Section 45, Grave S-45.

Anyway, with Mary holding all the cards, the Lincoln Monument Association quickly folded. Its members may have entertained second thoughts after a band of would-be bodysnatchers broke into the Lincoln tomb on election night, 1876. The conspirators planned to hide the presidential remains in an Indiana sand dune pending the release of their leader, who was in jail on counterfeiting charges. The intruders nearly succeeded in extricating the Great Emancipator's coffin before being surprised by agents who had infiltrated the gang.

Springfield, Illinois

This simple tombstone marks the second place Lincoln's body was interred

Over the next quarter century, Springfield's city fathers buried and reburied their most famous citizen.

At one point Lincoln's casket was concealed under construction materials, leaving admirers to pay homage before an empty tomb. In September 1901, a small group assembled at Oak Ridge; among those in attendance was a thirteen-year-old boy named Fleetwood Lindley, who had been hastily summoned to the scene by his father. A pungent odor filled the tomb as a blowtorch-wielding plumber removed the section of Lincoln's green lead casket above the president's head and shoulders.

Young Lindley crowded forward with the others to get a better look.

What they saw, thirty-six years after the fact, was the handiwork of a Philadelphia undertaker, who had used white chalk to disguise the decomposing corpse during its cross-country rail journey.

Notwithstanding this macabre cosmetic touch, Lincoln's features were plainly recognizable to the boy. To be sure, the presidential eyebrows had vanished and yellow mold and small red spots, the latter guessed to be remnants of an American flag, disfigured the black broadcloth suit in which Lincoln had taken his second inauguration oath in March 1865. But the figure in the coffin was unmistakably Abraham Lincoln. His identity established and the crowd's curiosity gratified, Lincoln was lowered for the final time into a cage of steel bars and smothered under ten feet of Portland cement. Before his death in 1963, Fleetwood Lindley claimed distinction as the last living person to have gazed upon the features of Abraham Lincoln.

— RNS

Andrew Johnson

Buried: Andrew Johnson National Cemetery, Greeneville, Tennessee

Seventeenth President – 1865-1869

Born: December 29, 1808, in Raleigh, North Carolina

Died: 2:30 a.m. on July 31, 1875, in Carter County, Tennessee

Age at death: 66

Cause of death: Stroke

Final words: Unknown

Admission to Andrew Johnson National Cemetery: Free

Even after winning the presidency, Andrew Johnson viewed himself as a common man. Born into poverty, Johnson opened his own tailor shop when he was seventeen. The next year he met and married Eliza McCardle, who taught him to read and write. Although he had no formal schooling, Johnson worked his way up through elective offices in his home state of Tennessee and in the U.S. Congress. In 1865, he became vice president under Abraham Lincoln.

Thrust into the presidency upon Lincoln's assassination, Andrew Johnson served a single term largely occupied with the reconstruction of the South after the Civil War. The first president to be impeached, he was acquitted in the Senate by just one vote. Andrew Johnson was not renominated by his party for a second term, but he was welcomed home with

Greeneville, Tennessee

honors to Greeneville, Tennessee. He
remained active in Democratic Party
politics, campaigning on behalf of other
candidates and even seeking further
elective office himself. In 1874, he was
elected to the U.S. Senate, the only
former president to serve there.

Andrew Johnson's tomb

A cholera epidemic devastated
much of the southern United States in
1873. Andrew Johnson caught the
disease and recovered, but never fully
regained his strength. In June of that year, sensing he was failing, he
wrote, "I have performed my duty to my God, my country, and my
family. I have nothing to fear in approaching death. To me it is the mere
shadow of God's protecting wing."

On July 28, 1875, Johnson and his wife were visiting their daughter
in Carter County, Tennessee, when he suffered a stroke that left his right
side paralyzed. He regained consciousness the next day, but refused to
seek the treatment of a doctor or the comfort of a minister. The
following day he suffered a second stroke which left him unable to
speak. Surrounded by family, Johnson died at his daughter's home on
July 31, 1875. His body was placed in a simple pine casket packed with
ice to counter the sun's sweltering rays. A public forum was held that
evening in Nashville for citizens to express their condolences.

Johnson's body was taken to lie in state at the Greeneville courthouse
on August 2. The town, including Johnson's old tailor shop, was draped in
black. At his request, Johnson's body was wrapped in the American flag,
his head rested on a copy of the Constitution. His body had already begun
to decompose in the extreme heat, so the casket remained closed.
Tennessee Governor James Porter was among the dignitaries who paid
their respects. In cities across the country, federal offices were closed and
flags were flown at half mast in Johnson's honor.

The next day under cloudy skies, five thousand people and a small
honor guard escorted the casket to his gravesite where a simple Masonic
funeral service was held. Andrew Johnson was buried on top of a hill on

Andrew Johnson

land he owned in Greeneville. He chose the site himself, marking it with a seedling reportedly taken from a willow tree near Napoleon's St. Helena deathbed. His wife Eliza was buried beside him when she died six months later.

Touring the Tomb at the Andrew Johnson National Historic Site

Andrew Johnson's gravesite is part of the Andrew Johnson National Historic Site in Greeneville, Tennessee. The site is open daily from 9:00 a.m. to 5:00 p.m., and is closed on Thanksgiving, Christmas, and New Year's Day. Admission to the gravesite is free, and includes a guided tour of the homestead. Visitors under age eighteen or over sixty-one are admitted to the homestead for free.

To reach the site from the north: Take Interstate 81 South to exit 36, then Route 172 South to Greeneville. Follow the signs to the visitors center, located at the corner of College and Depot Streets in Greeneville.

From the south: Take Interstate 81 North to exit 23, then Route 11E north to Greeneville. Follow the signs to the visitor center, located at the corner of College and Depot Streets in Greeneville.

To reach the cemetery from the visitor's center, go north on College Street to McKee Street. Turn east on McKee Street. Take McKee Street to Main Street. From Main Street, head south two blocks, and turn left on Monument Avenue. The cemetery is at the top of Monument Avenue.

At the cemetery entrance, turn right. Take the road up the hill. President Johnson's gravesite is located on top of the hill and is designated with a large, white landmark.

This plaque at the Andrew Johnson National Historic site tells the story of Johnson's funeral

For additional information

Andrew Johnson National Historic Site
121 Monument Avenue
Greeneville, TN 37743
Phone: (423) 638-3551
Fax: (423) 638-9194
www.nps.gov/anjo/

ABOVE: Abraham Lincoln's final resting place at Oak Ridge Cemetery in Springfield, Illinois.

PREVIOUS PAGE: This bronze bust of Abraham Lincoln stands near his tomb. Visitors rub its nose for good luck.

OPPOSITE: Lincoln's marble sarcophagus. His wife Mary and three of their children are buried across from him.

ABOVE: Andrew Johnson's funeral monument in Greeneville, Tennessee has a marble eagle perched on top and a stone flag wrapped around its column. The words of the Constitution are carved at its base.

OPPOSITE: Grant's tomb at Riverside Drive and 122nd Street in New York City.

ABOVE: Rutherford B. Hayes's tomb was constructed with granite mined from his father's farm in Dummerston, Vermont. It is located on the grounds of his Spiegel Grove estate in Fremont, Ohio.

OPPOSITE: Light filters through stained glass windows onto James Garfield's marble statue in his Cleveland, Ohio tomb.

A bronze Angel of Sorrow rests its arm on Chester Arthur's grave at Albany Rural Cemetery, just outside Albany, New York.

"To admirers, he was 'the Old Commoner,' to critics, a hopeless relic..." —*Richard Norton Smith*

The president who proposed Restoration instead of Reconstruction was himself restored to his pre-war place in the Senate by fellow Tennesseeans, most of whom shared his racial and economic views. To admirers, he was "the Old Commoner," to critics, a hopeless relic who single-handedly thwarted the cause of racial justice while squandering the moral high ground purchased with northern blood. "Pillow my head with the Constitution of my country," Johnson directed his executors. "Let the flag of the Nation be my winding sheet." His wishes were carried out to the letter.

Andrew Johnson selected the spot where his marble tomb now stands

On the eve of his funeral, Johnson's old tailor shop in Greeneville was festooned in mourning cloth. So was the Court House where thousands of plain people—his constituency of the dispossessed—came to pay their respects to the workingman's president. Today his grave is marked by a marble shaft atop which perches an American eagle. A billowing stone flag drapes part of the monument. The words of the Constitution are carved into its side, above the simple, generous tribute, even more debatable than most such graveyard summations: "His faith in the people never wavered."

— RNS

Ulysses S. Grant

Buried: General Grant National Memorial, New York, New York

Eighteenth President – 1869-1877

Born: April 27, 1822, in Point Pleasant, Ohio

Died: 8:06 a.m. on July 23, 1885, in Mount McGregor, New York

Age at death: 63

Cause of death: Throat cancer

Final words: "Water."

Admission to General Grant National Memorial: Free

Ulysses S. Grant, hero of the Civil War's battlefields, was terrified in the presence of animal blood. So consuming was his fear that he ordered steaks extra-well done. Grant's squeamishness did not extend to the front lines. His military leadership won him the Republican nomination for president in 1868. The war and scandal-weary nation hoped the general could restore peace.

Following his two terms as president, Grant embarked in 1877 on an ambitious two-year tour of the world with his wife Julia and son Jesse. He met with several heads of state, including Queen Victoria, and later cooperated in documenting the tour in a book. When he returned, Grant settled in Galena, Illinois. In 1880 he led the field for the Republican nomination for the presidency. James Garfield

Entrance to Grant's Tomb on Riverside Drive and 122nd Street in New York City

edged out the former president by just sixty-six votes, thus preventing Grant from becoming the first person to be nominated for a third term. Grant's luck worsened when a series of schemes in which he invested failed, leaving him penniless and publicly humiliated.

After he complained of frequent sore throats in the spring of 1884, doctors ordered the general, a lifelong cigar smoker, to stop smoking. The following year he began to lose his voice and had trouble swallowing. Doctors diagnosed cancer of the throat. Grant had such difficulty swallowing food that by the following spring he'd lost nearly seventy-five pounds, almost half his weight. His doctors treated him with a mixture of pain-relieving drugs—morphine and cocaine, to which the former president gradually became addicted. He soon lost the ability to speak above a whisper and communicated primarily with notes. His coughing fits grew so bad that Grant was frequently forced to sleep sitting up in a chair so as not to choke to death. During those many sleepless nights, Grant began work on his autobiography.

In June of 1885, Grant moved from New York City to Mount McGregor, New York, to continue work on his memoirs; he hoped to earn enough money to leave his wife financially secure after his death. Yet within a month, his health took a turn for the worse. By July 22, Ulysses Grant was fading in and out of consciousness. He opened his eyes when his wife spoke to him and in one of his final statements said,

Ulysses S. Grant

"I don't want anybody to feel distressed on my account." His only spoken word after that was a request for water. After suffering increasing difficulty breathing, doctors gave him brandy for the pain and applied hot cloths to warm his extremities.

The scene surrounding Grant's deathbed was a crowded one. In addition to his family, several doctors, nurses, a minister, a stenographer, and a sculptor (for the death mask) gathered around the dying man in the parlor of his home. When he died on the morning of July 23, the first news reports were on the wire within two minutes.

After he became ill, Grant had considered three potential sites for his burial: West Point, eliminated because the academy would not allow his wife to be buried with him; Galena, Illinois, where he received his first general's commission; and New York City. Unknown to the general, his family had also discussed burial at the Old Soldiers' Home in Washington, D.C. Ultimately, a site was recommended overlooking the Hudson River on the Upper West Side of Manhattan. Here, he was laid to rest on August 8, 1885, following one of the largest pageants the country had ever witnessed: sixty thousand people marched in his funeral procession.

New York City's African-American population played a leading role in the initial planning and funding for Grant's tomb. Richard Greener, the first black graduate of Harvard, was secretary of the Grant Monument Association. In 1888, he organized a design competition to gather proposals from architects for a suitable monument. The winner was an elaborate granite and white marble tomb designed by John Duncan. The tomb, which broke with the then-current fashion of erecting obelisks, was completed in 1897 and dedicated by President William McKinley in a ceremony attended by a crowd estimated at one million people. It is the largest mausoleum in North America. Grant's wife Julia was buried alongside him when she died in 1902.

Touring Ulysses S. Grant's Tomb at the General Grant National Memorial

After years of disrepair, the General Grant National Memorial is now restored. Operated by the National Park Service, the memorial is located at Riverside Drive and 122nd Street in New York City on the Upper West Side of Manhattan. Operating hours are from 9:00 a.m. to 5:00 p.m., daily, except New Year's Day, Thanksgiving Day, and Christmas. Admission is free.

To reach the memorial by car: Take the Henry Hudson Parkway to the 95th Street exit. Go north on Riverside Drive to 122nd Street. A limited amount of street parking is available.

To reach the memorial by subway: Take the Seventh Avenue–Broadway #1 subway train, which stops at the West 116th Street station on Broadway, two blocks east and six blocks south of Grant's Tomb.

Bus service is provided on Riverside Drive up to 120th Street by route M-5. To reach the memorial by bus: Take the M11 bus to Amsterdam Avenue and West 118th Street.

For additional information

Superintendent
General Grant National Memorial
Riverside Drive and 122nd Street
New York, NY 10003
Phone: (212) 932-9631
Fax: (212) 666-1679
www.nps.gov/gegr

"Doctors applied a cocaine solution to dull the excruciating pain of throat cancer, the result of Grant's twenty-cigar-a-day habit."

—Richard Norton Smith

In fact, there is nothing new about fascination with death, especially as it affects the politically celebrated who can outrun any opponent but time. In the summer of 1885, Ulysses S. Grant died by inches while an eager public camped outside the twelve-room cottage on New York's Mount McGregor. Inside the old hero was attempting to recoup his losses from a Wall Street swindle by penning his war memoirs for Mark Twain.

Doctors applied a cocaine solution to dull the excruciating pain of throat cancer, the result of Grant's twenty-cigar-a-day habit. Nightly injections of morphine enabled the patient to gain strength for the next day's incessant scribbling. As the death watch dragged on, knots of curiosity seekers climbed the wooded mountain slope to observe the general on his front porch, a skeletal figure in top hat and shawls, conjuring memories of Vicksburg

and the Wilderness while gazing off toward the Saratoga battlefield.

When the disease permanently silenced verbal communication, Grant scrawled a poignantly humorous note to his doctors. "I think I am a verb instead of a personal pronoun. A verb is anything that signifies to be; to do; or to suffer. I think I signify all three."

Nor did this marvelous Victorian melodrama end with Grant's death on July 23, 1885. Too many old soldiers had too much invested in their commander's glory, and glorification, to consign him to a temporary vault on 122nd Street. Hard times slowed the effort to build a shrine worthy of the Union's military savior, as did a rival campaign to install the Statue of Liberty on her pedestal in New York harbor.

In 1890, the Senate passed a bill to remove Grant's remains to Arlington National Cemetery, a step staunchly opposed by the general's widow, Julia. Whatever their motive,

Ulysses S. Grant and his wife Julia lie side by side in Grant's mammoth marble tomb

the lawmakers succeeded in prodding New York's dilatory fundraisers. On April 27, 1897, Grant's seventy-fifth birthday, a million people lined the streets of Manhattan to watch aging warriors of the Grand Army of the Republic and ambassadors from twenty-seven nations join President McKinley in dedicating the largest mausoleum in America.

To the novelist Henry James, Grant's Tomb symbolized "democracy in the all together…an unguarded shrine where all could come and go at their own will." Inside, beneath mosaics depicting his martial triumphs, the general and his lady lie in twin ten-ton sarcophogi carved from Wisconsin porphyry, Julia having rejected the idea of a single monument. "General Grant must have his own sarcophagus, and I must have mine beside him," she explained. "Hereafter when persons visit this spot, they must be able to say 'here rests General Grant.'" If his presidency, crooked as a dog's hind leg, tarnished Grant's historical standing, it certainly hadn't diminished his hold on popular affections.

— RNS

Ulysses S. Grant

Rutherford B. Hayes

Buried: Hayes Presidential Center, Fremont, Ohio

Nineteenth President — 1877-1881

Born: October 4, 1822, in Delaware, Ohio

Died: 11:00 p.m. on January 17, 1893, in Fremont, Ohio

Age at death: 70

Cause of death: Heart attack

Final words: "I know I am going where Lucy is."

Admission to Hayes Presidential Center: $7.50

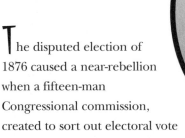

The disputed election of 1876 caused a near-rebellion when a fifteen-man Congressional commission, created to sort out electoral vote fraud, awarded the White House to Rutherford B. Hayes in a party-line vote. It earned Hayes, who had lost the popular vote, the derisive nickname "His Fraudulency."

Hayes had promised not to seek a second term. In March 1881, he attended the inauguration of his successor, James Garfield, and happily left Washington for retirement in his native Ohio. The Hayes's new life got off to an inauspicious start: the train in which they were traveling crashed, leaving two other passengers dead. Rutherford and Lucy Hayes were unhurt and continued the trip to Fremont and the home they had named Spiegel Grove.

In 1889, the much-admired Lucy Hayes suffered a series of strokes and died. The couple had been very close and

Hayes wrote in his diary, "The charm of life left me when Lucy died." He busied himself with public affairs, including service as a trustee of Cleveland's Case Western Reserve University.

In January of 1893, Hayes sat in a drafty train car en route to a university trustees meeting. Chilled, he felt ill throughout the meeting; at the station on his return to Fremont, Hayes suffered a heart attack.

Despite the concern of others, Hayes downed some brandy to restore his spirits and boarded the train for home. There, his doctor ordered the former president to his bed and for a while, Hayes seemed to improve. But on January 17, Hayes's heart gave out; he died in the arms of his second son Webb, telling him, "I know I'm going where Lucy is." Hayes was seventy.

News of Hayes's death reached Washington. Outgoing President Benjamin Harrison issued a proclamation in honor of Hayes and ordered flags to fly half-staff. Harrison, a fellow Republican, elected not to make the trip to Fremont for Hayes's funeral, although the incoming president, Grover Cleveland—a Democrat—did.

January weather in Ohio was bitter cold. The streets were covered in snow. Yet thousands of mourners, including Ohio governor and future president William McKinley, turned out. Public schools and businesses closed in honor of the former president.

Hayes's body lay in state in Spiegel Grove's dining room. Dozens of floral arrangements surrounded his cedar coffin and a large American flag covered one wall of the room. When the service began on the afternoon of January 20, the house was jammed with visitors. The Reverend J.W. Bashford, a friend of forty years who had married Rutherford and Lucy, read the 23rd Psalm and prayed for the dead president. In deference to the freezing weather, a brief military ceremony was also conducted inside the home. Veterans of Hayes's 23rd Ohio Regiment served as pallbearers, escorting the casket to Fremont's Oakwood Cemetery, where Hayes was buried next to Lucy.

In 1910, Hayes's son Webb donated Spiegel Grove to the state of Ohio. The Hayes Presidential Center, the nation's first presidential library, was established at the site. On April 3, 1915, the bodies of the former president and first lady were re-interred at Spiegel Grove, on a site just south of the family home. Their tomb was constructed of granite mined from Hayes's father's farm in Dummerston, Vermont. A marble headstone,

Rutherford B. Hayes

designed for Lucy by Hayes, was also moved to Spiegel Grove. The stone was so heavy, a temporary rail line had to be constructed to move the stone to its new location.

The burial site for two of Rutherford Hayes's horses, "Old Ned" and "Old Whitey," can be found just outside the fence surrounding the presidential tomb.

Touring Rutherford B. Hayes's Tomb at the Hayes Presidential Center

The Hayes Presidential Center is located in Fremont, Ohio, on the grounds of Spiegel Grove, the Hayes's twenty-five-acre estate. It is open Tuesday through Sunday and closed Easter, Thanksgiving, Christmas, and New Year's Day. Hours are from 9:00 a.m. to 5:00 p.m., Tuesday through Saturday, and noon to 5:00 p.m. on Sundays and holidays. The library is closed on Sundays and holidays. Admission to the museum and home is $7.50 for adults, $6.50 for senior citizens, and $3.00 for children ages six to twelve. Admission for children under six is free. Special rates are available for groups. Visits to the gravesite are free. The grave is located on the south side of the Hayes home.

From the east or west: From the Ohio Turnpike (I-80/90), take exit 91/6. After leaving the turnpike, follow the signs for State Route 53-South. (This will take you onto the US 20 Bypass briefly, then back onto SR 53-South.) After approximately five miles, you will come to the junction of State Route 6-West. Turn left at the light (which is Hayes Avenue, but is not labeled). After the second light on Hayes Avenue, look for a flashing yellow light, about 2.2 miles from US 6. Turn right and immediately make a second right into the Rutherford B. Hayes Presidential Center. The entrance to the center is at the corner of Hayes and Buckland Avenues. From the city of Fremont, follow the brown and white Hayes Presidential Center signs.

Stone marker at the Hayes Presidential Center

For additional information

The Rutherford B. Hayes Presidential Center
Spiegel Grove
Fremont, Ohio 43420-2796
Phone: (419) 332-2081 / (800) 998-7737
Fax: (419) 332-4952
www.rbhayes.org

"...Hayes proved to be the gold in the Gilded Age..." —*Richard Norton Smith*

*E*levated to the White House in 1876 amid rancorous cries of electoral fraud, Hayes proved to be the gold in the Gilded Age, a foe of the spoils system and a dedicated teetotaler whose feminist wife won immortality, and patronization, as "Lemonade Lucy." Time was on their side: less than a year after leaving office, Hayes helped to bury the assassinated Garfield. In the summer of 1885, he rode in Grant's funeral procession, sharing a carriage with none other than Chester Arthur, the onetime boss of the New York Customhouse whose removal Hayes had orchestrated, and who had gone on, against all odds, to become an effective reformer in his own right.

In June 1889, Hayes lost his greatest friend. "How easily I could let go of life," he said in the wake of Lucy's passing. On a Sunday in January 1893, he visited her grave in the cemetery near his handsome estate called Spiegel Grove. That evening he wrote in his diary of his longing to join her. At the Cleveland train station a few days later, Hayes

Roger Bridges, former director of the Hayes Presidential Center, with C-SPAN consulting historian John Splaine at the Hayes tomb

experienced severe chest pains. "I would rather die at Spiegel Grove," he said, "than to live anywhere else."

On the night of January 17, his wish was granted. President-elect Grover Cleveland made the long train journey from Washington to attend Hayes's funeral. "He was coming to see me," said Cleveland. "But he is dead and I will go to see him." The gesture would have touched Hayes, for, by his gallant action, Cleveland buried all the old charges about the disputed election of 1876, along with the man who had won it.

— *RNS*

James A. Garfield

Buried: Lake View Cemetery, Cleveland, Ohio

Twentieth President – 1881

Born: November 19, 1831, in Orange, Ohio

Died: 10:35 p.m. on September 19, 1881, in Elberon, New Jersey

Age at death: 49

Cause of death: Infection resulting from assassin's bullet

Final words: "Oh, Swaim, there is a pain here. Oh, Swaim!"
(to David Gaskill Swaim, his chief of staff)

Admission to Lake View Cemetery: Free

Medical incompetence may have been partially to blame for the death of the twentieth president. Clean instruments and a different sickbed might have prolonged James Garfield's life.

On July 2, 1881, Garfield became the second president to be wounded seriously while in office. Four months into his term, Garfield, accompanied by Secretary of State James Blaine, set off for a trip to the Northeast. As Garfield and Blaine walked arm-in-arm through Washington's Baltimore and Potomac railroad station (now the site of the National Gallery of Art) at about 9:30 a.m., a man came within a yard of the president and shot him twice with a .44-caliber British Bulldog pistol.

The first bullet superficially wounded Garfield's right arm. The second shot passed through his lower back and lodged

The Garfield Monument houses the remains of James and Lucretia Garfield

deep in his body. Garfield cried out, "My God, my God, what is this?" and fell, bleeding heavily. A doctor was on the scene within moments.

The assassin, Charles Julius Guiteau, was arrested at the station. A former Garfield supporter, he unsuccessfully sought a patronage position from the president and secretary of state. Turned down, he began shadowing the president. In the weeks prior to the shooting, Guiteau had come within range of the president three times—each time, he found a reason not to shoot. Several letters were found in his pockets, including one which read, "The president's tragic death was a sad necessity, but it will unite the Republican party and save the Republic.... I had no ill will towards the president."

James A. Garfield

Moved to the White House, surrounded by a half dozen physicians, Garfield sipped brandy to ease the pain. Doctors trying to find the bullet probed the wound in Garfield's back with bare hands and unsterilized instruments. Their prognosis was grim; they did not expect the president to live through the night. Garfield's family gathered at his bedside. Garfield tried to cheer his sixteen-year-old son Jimmy, saying, "Don't be alarmed. The upper story is all right, it is only the hull that is a little damaged."

A metal detector invented by Alexander Graham Bell was used in an attempt to find the bullet, but failed due to the unforeseen attraction of metal springs in Garfield's bed; doctors were mystified as to why the machine made the president's body appear bullet-riddled. They operated three times to remove bone fragments and drain abscesses near the wound. Newspapers across the country carried daily updates on the president's condition.

On September 6, Garfield asked to be taken by special train to the New Jersey seaside. For a few days he seemed to be recuperating. But on September 19, 1881, he complained of severe pains near his heart and fell unconscious. James Garfield died at 10:35 that evening at age forty-nine. Bells tolled across the country announcing his death. Vice President Chester Arthur took the oath of office a few hours later at his home in New York City.

A three-hour autopsy discovered that the bullet's actual trajectory was nowhere near what doctors originally thought. That miscalculation and a blood infection caused by the lack of sterile procedures were factors in Garfield's death.

At a private viewing held at his home, friends of the late president were shocked by his emaciated appearance. The *New York Times* reported: "The President's face was shockingly ghastly. The skin was drawn tightly over the projecting bones, except on the forehead, where it was deeply corrugated. The lips were apart, disclosing set teeth. The hair and whiskers had whitened perceptibly. No signs of the swelling or incisions were visible, but the face was blotched and covered with black specks—the result, it is said, partly, of the taking of a plaster cast of the face last night."

Garfield's body was carried by train to Washington on Wednesday, September 21, and was escorted up Pennsylvania Avenue to the Capitol by Chester Arthur and former president Ulysses S. Grant. Garfield's body lay in state in the Capitol rotunda for two days.

On Monday, September 26, 1881, Garfield's body was taken to his hometown for burial in Cleveland's Lake View Cemetery. Artillerymen lifted the casket from its platform onto a carriage led by twelve black horses. Former President Rutherford B. Hayes, a fellow Ohioan, led the procession. As rain began to fall, a band played "Nearer My God, to Thee," and James Garfield's body was placed into the cemetery's public vault.

Nine years later, Garfield was re-interred in Lake View Cemetery at the site of the newly completed James A. Garfield Monument. His wife Lucretia was buried there in 1918.

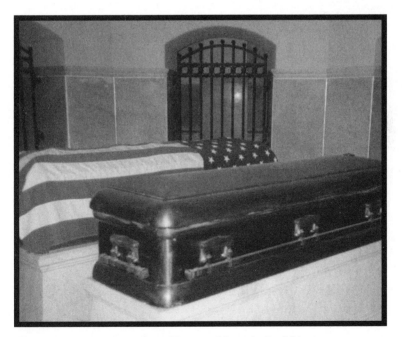

The crypt containing the caskets of James and Lucretia Garfield

James A. Garfield

Two months after James Garfield was buried, Charles Guiteau went on trial. Guiteau believed that God had ordered him to kill the president; his attorney (also his brother-in-law) argued that Guiteau was not guilty by reason of insanity. After an hour of deliberation, the jury found him guilty. Guiteau was sentenced to death. On his way to the gallows, Guiteau sang a hymn he had written about going to God. He was hanged before a crowd of spectators in Washington, D.C., on June 30, 1882.

Touring James Garfield's Tomb at Lake View Cemetery

The Lake View Cemetery is located in Cleveland, Ohio. The cemetery is open daily 7:30 a.m. to 5:30 p.m. The James A. Garfield Memorial Monument is open April 1 through the president's birthday, November 19, 9:00 a.m. to 4:00 p.m. Admission is free.

From Akron: Take I-480 northbound to I-271. Take I-271 North to the Mayfield Road exit. Go west on Mayfield Road for about four miles. The Mayfield gate of the cemetery is located at the intersection of Mayfield and Kenilworth Roads on the right.

From Toledo: Take I-90 East to exit 177. Take exit 177 to Martin Luther King, Jr. Drive. Turn left and proceed south for three miles to Euclid Avenue. Turn left on Euclid Avenue and drive east to the gates of Lake View Cemetery.

To reach the Garfield Monument, follow Garfield Road after entering the cemetery gates.

For additional information

Lake View Cemetery
12316 Euclid Avenue
Cleveland, Ohio 44106
Phone: (216) 421-2665
Fax: (216) 421-2415
www.lakeviewcemetery.com

"One hundred thousand mourners paid their respects to the late president..."

—Richard Norton Smith

Whether Garfield died at the hands of an assassin, or from the unsanitary probings of his doctors, remains a topic of scholarly debate. Beyond question was the depth of popular grief occasioned by his passing. One hundred thousand mourners paid their respects to the late president as he lay in state in the Capitol Rotunda; another twenty thousand requested tickets for Guiteau's hanging. In the aftermath, Congress enacted civil service legislation, much as lawmakers eight decades later would be shamed into passing a civil rights bill associated with the martyred John F. Kennedy.

That is not all Guiteau's crime inspired, as any visitor to Cleveland's Lake View Cemetery can see for himself. Part of a distinguished company that includes John D. Rockefeller, Mark Hanna, and John Hay, the twentieth president rests in a turreted red sandstone tower soaring 180 feet into the air. Beneath Memorial Hall, whose ornate mosaics and elegant

One of Garfield's neighbors in Lake View Cemetery

tilework have recently been restored to their original splendor, a nineteen-foot white Carrara marble Garfield stands forever poised on the edge of a campaign oration. Downstairs a crypt holds the caskets of the president and his wife, Lucretia. Forget the Rock and Roll Hall of Fame; when in Cleveland, head for Lake View.

— RNS

James A. Garfield

Chester Arthur

Buried: Albany Rural Cemetery, Albany, New York

Twenty-first President — 1881-1885

Born: October 5, 1829, in Fairfield, Vermont

Died: 5:00 a.m. on November 18, 1886, in New York, New York

Age at death: 57

Cause of death: Stroke

Final words: Unknown

Admission to Albany Rural Cemetery: Free

The circumstances surrounding Chester Arthur's birth nearly cost him the presidency. Arthur was born the son of a Baptist minister in Fairfield, Vermont. His political enemies knew that one way to keep Arthur out of the presidency was to prove he was born in Canada rather than Vermont, thus making him ineligible to be president. Though such charges followed him throughout the campaign of 1880, evidence that he was in fact Canadian was never provided.

The vice presidency under James Garfield was Arthur's first elective office. Arthur had not gotten over his wife Nell's recent death from pneumonia when James Garfield was assassinated in 1881. When he was president, Arthur hung Nell's portrait in the White House and insisted that fresh flowers be placed underneath it each day. Ironically, Arthur was

The Angel of Sorrow at the Arthur tomb

himself seriously ill, suffering from Bright's disease, a kidney ailment that left him feeling extremely fatigued. Reports of his condition, which Arthur steadfastly denied, appeared occasionally in the press.

Due to his illness, Arthur was not enthusiastic about another term but nevertheless sought his party's nomination. He was unsuccessful, losing the nomination to James G. Blaine. His health rapidly declined; by the later months of 1886, the former president was bedridden at his home in New York City, unable to eat solid food. Arthur remained optimistic, filling his days with books, newspapers, and visitors. His condition worsened after he was taken on a long ride through Central Park; Arthur never fully recovered. About two weeks before his death, Arthur fell into a state of depression and ordered all of his personal papers burned.

On the night of November 16, 1886, Chester Arthur suffered a severe stroke. A maid who came to wake him the next morning found him partially paralyzed and unable to speak. He soon fell unconscious. He died on November 18 in his home at 123 Lexington Avenue. A doctor and Arthur's two sisters were at his bedside; his daughter and nephew nearby. Telegrams were sent to the former president's other relatives and the surviving members of his cabinet, and an undertaker was summoned. Although many mourners came to pay their respects, the family remained in seclusion.

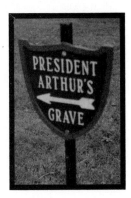

Chester Arthur

His funeral was held at 9:00 a.m. on November 22 at the Church of the Heavenly Rest on Fifth Avenue in New York City. As the family wished, it was a simple service with only a small military honor guard. Flags throughout the city were lowered to half staff, and many public and private buildings were draped in mourning. President Grover Cleveland attended. Pallbearers included Robert Todd Lincoln, Charles Louis Tiffany, and Cornelius Vanderbilt. Arthur's body was taken to Albany Rural Cemetery in Menands, New York, for burial. His elaborate tomb lies to the right of his beloved wife Nell's in the Arthur family plot.

Touring Chester Arthur's Tomb at Albany Rural Cemetery

The Albany Rural Cemetery is located in Menands, New York. The cemetery is open from 8:00 a.m. to 5:00 p.m. (6:00 p.m. during the summer months). Admission is free.

From Saratoga Springs: Take I-87 South to Alternate Route 7. From Alternate Route 7, head east to Highway 787. Take Highway 787 South to exit 7 west. Bear right, heading towards Menands/Loundenville. At the first traffic signal, take a right. Albany Rural Cemetery is located on the left.

From Utica: Take I-90 East to exit 24. From exit 24 continue on I-90 East to Highway 787 North. Take Highway 787 North to exit 7 West. From exit 7 West follow Route 32. Turn right on Route 32. Albany Rural Cemetery is on the left.

Look for red, white, and blue signs marking President Arthur's gravesite. Cemetery maps are available at the gate.

For additional information

Albany Rural Cemetery
Cemetery Avenue
Menands, NY 12204
Phone: (518) 463-7017
Fax: (518) 463-0785

The entrance to Chester Arthur's final resting place

"An elegant New Yorker, Chester A. Arthur refused to move into the shabby Executive Mansion..."

—Richard Norton Smith

An elegant New Yorker, Chester A. Arthur refused to move into the shabby Executive Mansion pending its extensive renovation by Louis Tiffany. Soon the old house was replete with pomegranate plush hangings and jeweled glass screens. To the abstemious Rutherford B. Hayes, Arthur's White House reeked of "liquor, snobbery and worse."

Arthur indulged his stylish tastes more permanently in the autumn of 1886, when Cornelius Vanderbilt's private railroad car carried the former president to Rural Cemetery in Albany. There his grave is marked by a black granite sarcophagus over which a bronze Angel of Sorrow, green-tinted with age, stands vigil.

— RNS

Plaque at the base of the Arthur tomb

Chester Arthur

Grover Cleveland

Buried: Princeton Cemetery, Princeton, New Jersey

Twenty-second President – 1885-1889
                    –and–
Twenty-fourth President – 1893-1897
Born: March 18, 1837, in Caldwell, New Jersey
Died: 8:40 a.m. on June 24, 1908, in Princeton, New Jersey
Age at death: 71
Cause of death: Heart failure
Final words: "I have tried so hard to do right."
Admission to Princeton Cemetery: Free

Grover Cleveland is remembered for four unusual reasons: He was the only president to serve two non-consecutive terms, as our twenty-second and twenty-fourth president. He was the only president to marry in the White House, where he wed Frances Folsom, twenty-eight years his junior. He was the only president to support an out-of-wedlock child—the opposition's 1884 campaign slogan, "Ma, Ma, where's my Pa?" nearly costing him the election. Finally, he was the only president to have a popular candy bar named after his daughter, Baby Ruth.

Grover Cleveland also had one medical distinction: he was the only president with a rubber jaw. During his second term, on a boat in Manhattan's East River, doctors secretly performed surgery to remove a cancerous tumor in Cleveland's mouth. His upper left jaw was removed and

replaced with a rubber prosthesis. The
details of the operation were not made
known until after Cleveland's death.

Cleveland retired to Princeton, New
Jersey, after leaving the White House for
the final time in 1897. He fell victim to
medical difficulties in his later years:
inflamed kidneys, swollen joints, blood
clots in the lungs, and dropsy.

Stomach problems caused such pain
that he had to learn how to use a pump to
clear his digestive tract. By the spring of
1908, his condition began to deteriorate
rapidly. Cleveland and his wife decided to
send their four young children to the care
of her mother at the Cleveland summer
home in Tamworth, New Hampshire.

*Grover Cleveland's grave in
Princeton Cemetery*

When he was able to get out of bed, the former president worked in a
study adjoining the bedroom of his home in Princeton.

On June 23, Grover Cleveland began to lapse in and out of
consciousness. Even during lucid moments, he remained weak. His last
words were, "I have tried so hard to do right." At 8:40 the following morning,
his heart gave out. His wife, a nurse, and three doctors were at his side.

On June 26 in keeping with Cleveland's wishes, an exceptionally
simple funeral service for less than one hundred guests was held at his
home. The body was brought downstairs to the reception room in a
closed casket where it was surrounded by palm leaves and floral tributes.
The mourners, including President Theodore Roosevelt and his wife,
assembled in the adjoining library. There was no eulogy and no music.
Instead, Presbyterian ministers recited prayers and read William
Wordsworth's poem "Character of the Happy Warrior."

Thirty minutes after the service began, the procession departed
to Princeton Cemetery under sunny skies. Crowds along the route
were smaller than expected—estimated at about five thousand.
The pallbearers walked on either side of the hearse, followed by
twenty-six carriages carrying the late president's family and friends. After

Grover Cleveland

a brief graveside ceremony, Grover Cleveland was buried alongside his thirteen-year-old daughter, Ruth, who had died two years before. Frances Folsom Cleveland lived until 1947; she was buried next to her husband.

Touring Grover Cleveland's Tomb at Princeton Cemetery

Princeton Cemetery is located in Princeton, New Jersey. The cemetery is always open, but prefers visitors during daylight hours.

From Trenton: Take Route 1 North to Route 571/Washington Road and head north. At the traffic circle, bear right and drive straight on Washington Road to Route 27/Nassau Street. Take a left on Nassau Street and turn left on Greenview Avenue and follow through gates of the cemetery.

From Philadelphia: Take I-95 North to Route 206. Drive north on Route 206. Continue on Route 206, passing the Governor's Mansion. At Library Place Street, continue straight ahead. Route 27 becomes Nassau Street/21. Turn left on Witherspoon Street. Continue on to next traffic light and turn right on Wiggins. Turn left on Greenview Avenue and follow through gates of the cemetery.

After you go through Princeton Cemetery's public gate a map box is located to your left. Grover Cleveland's grave is located across the walkway from the Old Graveyard. His plot is numbered nine on the cemetery map.

Also buried at Princeton Cemetery are John Witherspoon, a signer of

the Declaration of Independence and member of the Continental Congress, and Aaron Burr, the vice president famous for his duel with Alexander Hamilton.

For additional information

Superintendent
Princeton Cemetery
29 Greenview Avenue
Princeton, NJ 08542
Phone: (609) 924-1369

The headstone of Cleveland's thirteen-year-old daughter Ruth

"...tragedy struck the Cleveland household when the family's eldest daughter, Ruth, died..."

—*Richard Norton Smith*

In 1896, during the last year of his difficult second term, Cleveland was prevailed upon to visit Princeton University as part of the school's sesquicentennial observance. The academic program was organized by Dean Andrew West—"Andy Three Million West, sixty-three inches around the chest"—who became one of Cleveland's closest friends. On moving to Princeton in 1897, ex-president Cleveland built a substantial home he called Westland. Ironically, the star of the sesquicentennial was Woodrow Wilson, a rising faculty member who, in 1902, succeeded to the university's presidency. For a time, harmony prevailed—not surprising, given Wilson's conservative Democratic leanings and open admiration for Cleveland.

In January 1904 tragedy struck the Cleveland household when the family's eldest daughter, Ruth, died from diphtheria. "I had a season of great trouble in keeping out of my mind the idea that Ruth was in the cold, cheerless grave instead of in the arms of her Savior," wrote Cleveland. In time, however, his faith reasserted itself. God had come to his help, Cleveland told intimates, enabling him "to adjust my thought to dear Ruth's death with as much comfort as selfish humanity will permit."

Another kind of crisis engulfed the grieving parent as Wilson and Dean West clashed over West's proposal for a new graduate college at Princeton. Cleveland aligned himself with the tradition-loving dean, leading to an estrangement between the once and future presidents. As Cleveland lay on his death bed in the spring of 1908, he summoned West to reiterate his support for the dean's plans. "Hang on to it like a bulldog," the dying Cleveland told West, "no matter what is done to you." By then he had come to regard Wilson as thoroughly unreliable.

For his part, the beleaguered Wilson declared that Cleveland was "a better president of the United States than a trustee of Princeton." It was a sad climax to their once promising friendship, and a preview of Wilson's unyielding stand a decade later on the League of Nations.

— RNS

Grover Cleveland

Benjamin Harrison

Buried: Crown Hill Cemetery, Indianapolis, Indiana

Twenty-third President – 1889-1893

Born: August 20, 1833, in North Bend, Ohio

Died: 4:45 p.m. on March 13, 1901, in Indianapolis, Indiana

Age at death: 67

Cause of death: Pneumonia

Final words: "Are the doctors here?"

"Doctor, ...my lungs"

Admission to Crown Hill Cemetery: Free

Benjamin Harrison, grandson of ninth president William Henry Harrison, served his single term between the two terms of Grover Cleveland. In the 1888 election, Harrison actually lost to Republican Cleveland in the popular vote, but won the majority of the electoral votes. His term saw the admission of six states to the union and the addition of electric lights to the White House.

Caroline Harrison, the new president's wife, began the tradition of displaying a White House Christmas tree as her husband's first year in office drew to a close. After supervising major renovations to the executive mansion, she died of tuberculosis during his reelection campaign.

After losing his second bid for the presidency in 1892, Benjamin Harrison began an active second career as a lawyer, writer, and professor. He also remarried at age sixty-two to

Benjamin Harrison's tomb

Mary Dimmick, a niece of his late wife who had worked as an assistant to the First Lady.

In March of 1901 at age sixty-seven, Harrison took ill at his home in Indianapolis. A simple case of the flu turned into pneumonia. Harrison did not respond to various treatments and on March 12 lapsed in and out of a coma. His relatives and closest friends gathered by his bedside. At about 4:45 p.m. on March 13, 1901, Benjamin Harrison died.

On March 16, Harrison's body was taken to lie in state in the rotunda of the Indiana state capitol. A small private service was performed at his home the next day. A larger funeral was held at the First Presbyterian Church where Harrison had been a member for nearly fifty years. Citizens lined up outside more than two hours before the service began. Mourners inside spilled over into the aisles, and the altar overflowed with roses, lilies, and violets. The church choir sang "Rock of Ages," reportedly the late president's favorite hymn—and the only one he ever tried to sing. President William McKinley was in attendance and members of Harrison's cabinet served as honorary pallbearers.

Benjamin Harrison was buried beside his first wife, Carrie, at Crown Hill Memorial Cemetery in Indianapolis. At the graveside service, three white carnations were placed on top of the walnut casket. The casket, enclosed in a granite tomb, was lowered into the ground to the sounds of cannon fire.

Touring Benjamin Harrison's Tomb at Crown Hill Cemetery

Crown Hill Cemetery is located in Indianapolis, Indiana. Crown Hill is also the burial site of three vice presidents: Thomas Riley Marshall, vice president to Woodrow Wilson, Thomas Andrews Hendricks, vice president to Grover Cleveland, and Charles Warren Fairbanks, vice president to Theodore Roosevelt.

Crown Hill Cemetery is open daily from 8:00 a.m. to 8:00 p.m., April 1 through October 14, and from 8:00 a.m. to 5:00 p.m., October 15 through March 31. The cemetery's office is open Monday through Friday, 8:00 a.m. to 5:00 p.m., and Saturday, 8:30 a.m. to 2:00 p.m. The office is closed Sundays and holidays. There is no admission fee.

From Indianapolis International Airport: Exit the airport and go east on I-70, toward downtown Indianapolis. Stay in the left lane as it merges into I-65 North. Exit on the right onto Meridian Street and turn right. Take Meridian Street north to Thirty-fourth Street. Turn left onto Thirty-fourth Street and follow it through two stop lights. Thirty-fourth Street will dead-end at the cemetery's large stone gate. This is the Thirty-fourth Street and Boulevard Place entrance. Follow the white line painted on the road to the president's memorial.

From downtown Indianapolis: Crown Hill Cemetery is approximately 3.6 miles from Monument Circle where Meridian and Market Streets intersect. Take Meridian Street north to Thirty-fourth Street. Turn left onto Thirty-fourth Street and follow it through two stop lights. Thirty-fourth Street will dead-end at the cemetery's large stone gate. This is the Thirty-fourth Street and Boulevard Place entrance.

A waiting station is located on the right at the Thirty-fourth Street and Boulevard Place entrance. There you will find cemetery maps with directions to President Harrison's gravesite. White lines on the cemetery road also lead to Harrison's grave.

Crown Hill Cemetery offers a two-hour tour that examines the life of Benjamin Harrison and other notables buried in the cemetery. The "Politicians" Tour is offered seven days a week from 8:00 a.m. to dusk. Admission is $5.00 for adults, $4.00 for seniors, and $3.00 for students, with a $50.00 minimum per private tour. (Visitors can schedule a private "Politicians" Tour by calling ahead.) Self-guided tours are free. One may purchase a $5.00 cemetery tour book from the main office from 8:30 a.m. to 5:00 p.m. Monday through Friday, 8:30 a.m. to 2:00 p.m. Saturday, and noon to 5:00 p.m. on Sunday.

For additional information

Crown Hill Cemetery
700 West 38th Street
Indianapolis, Indiana 46208
Cemetery office: (317) 925-3800
Tour information: (317) 920-2649 /
(800) 809-3366
Fax: (317) 925-8240
www.crownhillhf.org

"... 'the Harrison Horror' led Ohio's legislature to enact stringent laws against bodysnatchers."

—Richard Norton Smith

*B*enjamin Harrison, already overshadowed by his grandfather president—if anyone can be overshadowed by a man who held office barely a month—plays second fiddle to bank robber John Dillinger at Indianapolis Crown Hill Cemetery. At that, he is luckier than some other White House occupants, not to mention his own father, an Ohio congressman named John Scott Harrison. Soon after John Harrison's death in May 1878, his body was stolen from its grave by "resurrectionists" affiliated with the Ohio Medical College. A professor at that eminent institution did nothing to diminish public fury through

Harrison's tomb at Crown Hill Cemetery

his offhanded observation that graverobbing mattered little, "since it would all be the same on the day of the resurrection."

Benjamin Harrison led the charge against the college and its anatomical research practices. In an indignant public letter, the future president vividly described the sight of his father's body "hanging by the neck, like that of a dog, in a pit of a medical college." In time, John Scott Harrison was quietly reburied, the perpetrators tried and punished, and popular outrage over "the Harrison Horror" led Ohio's legislature to enact stringent laws against bodysnatchers.

— RNS

Caroline Harrison was the president's first wife

William McKinley

Twenty-fifth President – 1897-1901
Born: January 29, 1843, in Niles, Ohio
Died: 2:15 a.m. on September 14, 1901, in Buffalo, New York
Age at death: 58
Cause of death: Gangrene resulting from assassin's bullet
Final words: "It is God's way. His will be done, not ours. We are all going. . . . Oh, dear"
Admission to McKinley National Museum: $7.00

The election of 1896 pitted the fiery orator William Jennings Bryan against the genteel front-porch campaigner, William McKinley. The issue was money—and whether the U.S. currency would be backed by gold or silver. McKinley, supporting the gold standard and backed by the political organization and money of Ohio industrialist Mark Hanna, won a handy electoral college victory.

The 1898 explosion of the battleship *Maine* in the Havana harbor became a major factor in McKinley's decision to fight the Spanish-American War. Among its outcomes was the transfer of the Philippines, Guam, and Puerto Rico to the United States; Hawaii was annexed and the Boxer Rebellion was quelled in China with U.S. involvement.

Against this foreign policy background, Bryan and McKinley faced off again in 1900. Republican party insiders, hoping to send New York's noisy governor Theodore Roosevelt off to the oblivion of the vice presidency, chose him to join McKinley on the ticket.

Roosevelt served as vice president for just six months. In September 1901 McKinley traveled to Buffalo, New York, for the Pan-American Exposition. The easygoing, gregarious president looked forward to the opportunity to get out among the populace. McKinley's personal secretary, George Cortelyou, was more cautious. Fearing that such an open, uncontrolled event could prove dangerous, he cancelled the president's appearance without his knowledge. When McKinley got wind of the change, he insisted that he would attend as scheduled, saying, "No one would want to hurt me."

McKinley's confidence proved fatally misplaced. On September 6 after a pleasant day trip to Niagara Falls, he returned to the fair for yet another round of handshakes. The receiving line stretched between a row of more than two dozen guards—extra security to appease the president's aides.

In the crowd was an unemployed, disaffected young man named Leon Czolgosz, who had been trailing the president for days. As McKinley stepped forward to greet him, Czolgosz raised his bandaged right hand. The handkerchief wrapped around his hand concealed a .32-caliber revolver. He quickly fired two shots at the president's midsection. The first ricocheted and missed its intended target. The second ripped through McKinley's stomach.

The wounded president's first thoughts were of others. As his secretary and security detail rushed to his aid, he begged them to protect the fragile health of his wife Ida, a chronic invalid. He feared that she would be unable to cope with the news of the shooting. The crowd tackled Czolgosz. McKinley pleaded with them not to injure the gunman.

McKinley was taken by ambulance to a nearby hospital. Doctors operated to determine the bullet's trajectory. They deemed the president stable enough to recover at the home of his host, John Milburn, the Exposition's president. McKinley rested comfortably there and seemed to rally—so much that he requested solid food and a cigar.

William McKinley

Doctors allowed him the food, but after eating, the president took a turn for the worse. Doctors were unaware that gangrene had ravaged the president's wounded organs.

With his wife at his bedside, McKinley died at 2:15 a.m. on September 14, eight days after the shooting, becoming the third American president to die at the hands of an assassin. Theodore Roosevelt, on vacation in the Adirondacks, received a telegram with the news and raced to Buffalo. That afternoon, he was sworn in as the twenty-sixth president of the United States.

The funeral rites began with a private service at the Milburn home. The president's coffin lay in the drawing room, draped with an American flag and surrounded by floral arrangements. The new chief executive, Theodore Roosevelt, and various other dignitaries sat before the open casket. An impassive Ida McKinley listened from the top of the stairs.

At the service's end, the casket was placed onto a funeral carriage to the strains of the president's favorite hymn, "Nearer, My God, to Thee." The procession made its way through Buffalo, its streets lined with mourners. The president lay in state at the Buffalo City Hall, where more than two hundred thousand citizens lined up to pay their respects.

The next morning, the funeral train departed for Washington, D.C. Following the customs established by earlier presidential funerals, McKinley's body was returned to the White House before being taken down Pennsylvania Avenue to the Capitol. After lying in state in the Capitol Rotunda, the president's coffin was carried back to the funeral train for its final journey to his hometown. Neighbors and friends of the slain president attended a public service in Canton, Ohio. McKinley's remains were temporarily interred in the receiving vault at Westlawn Cemetery.

An outraged public called for Leon Czolgosz to be lynched. The self-described anarchist and admitted assassin was held in prison under tight security. Czolgosz was tried, convicted, and executed for McKinley's murder in less than two months.

The William McKinley National Memorial was completed in 1907, and his coffin was moved to its final resting place and enclosed in a dark green granite sarcophagus. Ida McKinley, who had died earlier that year, was buried alongside him.

The granite tombs of William and Ida McKinley

Touring William McKinley's Tomb at the McKinley National Memorial and Museum

The McKinley National Memorial and Museum is located in Canton, Ohio. It is open from 9:00 a.m. to 4:00 p.m., Monday through Saturday, and 12:00 p.m. to 4:00 p.m. on Sundays. The site is closed on major holidays and may be closed intermittently from December 1 to April 1. Visitors are advised to call for further information on hours of operation.

There is no admission fee to visit the McKinley Monument. Admission to the museum is $7.00 for adults, $6.00 for senior citizens, and $5.00 for children ages three to eighteen. Children under age three are admitted free.

From the north: Take I-77 South to exit 106 and follow the signs to the McKinley National Memorial and Museum.

From the south: Take I-77 North to exit 105 and follow the signs to the McKinley National Memorial and Museum.

For additional information

McKinley National Memorial and Museum
800 McKinley Monument Drive, NW
Canton, Ohio 44708
Phone: (330) 455-7043
www.mckinleymuseum.org

> ## "Elected on a staunchly protectionist platform, the last president of the nineteenth century came to anticipate many trends of the twentieth."
>
> —Richard Norton Smith

Americans like to think that the presidential office fosters growth in its occupants. (Woodrow Wilson more puckishly, and perhaps more accurately, observed that public men tend either to grow or swell.) William McKinley refutes the cynics. Elected on a staunchly protectionist platform, the last president of the nineteenth century came to anticipate many trends of the twentieth. A somewhat reluctant imperialist, McKinley saw the United States launched as a global power as a result of the Spanish-American War that brought the Philippines, Puerto Rico and (briefly) Cuba under American control.

Reelected in 1900, McKinley let it be known that he intended in his second term to break with tradition and visit his country's newly added foreign outposts. In a still more radical departure from his own past, McKinley told a large crowd at Buffalo's Pan-American Exposition in September 1901 that "isolation is no longer possible or desirable...the period of exclusiveness is past." In practical terms, this meant freer trade in place of the high tariff barriers of the past. McKinley the protectionist was transforming himself, almost overnight, into McKinley the internationalist.

His associates, concerned about security risks in an age of anarchist violence, urged the president to cancel a planned public reception at the fair. Knowing how much the kind-hearted McKinley hated to disappoint anyone, his

Canton, Ohio

personal secretary George Cortelyou tried another tack, reminding his boss that he couldn't possibly shake hands with all the thousands assembled to see him.

"Well, they'll know I tried, anyhow," McKinley told Cortelyou.

In the event, a group of uniformed soldiers, added as a precaution at the last minute, obstructed the view of the president's regular security staff, enabling Leon Czolgosz to get off two shots. "I didn't believe one man should have so much service, and another man should have none," explained the assassin. On the day of McKinley's funeral, the nation observed five minutes of silence. Secretary of State John Hay declared of the late president that he "showed in his life how a citizen should live, and in his last hour taught us how a great leader could die"—words that would echo over seventy years later in Walter Mondale's eulogy to his old friend Hubert Humphrey.

Ironically, the invalid Ida McKinley would outlive her husband by six years, during which the First Lady, who had been chronically ill, never again experienced one of the seizures that had cast a shadow over her married life.

—RNS

Theodore Roosevelt

Buried: Young's Memorial Cemetery, Oyster Bay, New York

Twenty-sixth President — 1901-1909

Born: October 27, 1858, in New York, New York

Died: 4:00 a.m. on January 6, 1919, in Oyster Bay, New York

Age at death: 60

Cause of death: Embolism

Final words: "James, will you please put out the light?"

Admission to Young's Memorial Cemetery: Free

Theodore Roosevelt, "Rough Rider," trust buster, Nobel Peace Prize winner, and champion of the Panama Canal, lived for ten years after leaving the White House and had one of the most active retirements of any president. Elected in his own right in 1904 after finishing McKinley's term, TR promised to retire after only a single full term in the White House. His hand-picked protégé, William Howard Taft, easily won the election of 1908.

After his successor's inauguration, Roosevelt returned to his Long Island home. He soon left the relative peace of Sagamore Hill to explore Africa. With an entourage numbering in the hundreds, Roosevelt and his son Kermit took a twelve-month safari, collecting samples of African wildlife for the Smithsonian Institution's collection.

Teddy Roosevelt's own words on a plaque near his grave

Returning to the United States in 1910, Roosevelt became convinced that President Taft had shifted too far to the right. He decided to challenge the incumbent. Falling short of winning the Republican nomination for president in 1912, he created the Progressive, or Bull Moose party, which split the GOP vote and put Woodrow Wilson in the White House. During the campaign, Roosevelt was the target of an assassination attempt by a deranged gunman. Shot in the chest, Roosevelt proceeded to give his scheduled speech before going to the hospital.

Over the next few years, TR continued to travel and write extensively. His lifelong passion for physical activity was his counterbalance for poor health, but his exertions caught up with him. He was hospitalized for a month in February 1918, following complications after emergency surgery on his leg. He never fully regained his balance. By the time he reached age sixty, TR was deaf in one ear, blind in one eye, and half-crippled with rheumatism. The pain in his joints grew so bad that his doctor ordered bed rest. TR disobeyed and was hospitalized a few days later. He remained in the hospital for seven weeks with his wife Edith by his side.

A considerably weakened Roosevelt returned home to his Sagamore Hill estate late in 1918. Devastated by the death of his youngest son Quentin in World War I, he spent most of his days

Theodore Roosevelt

resting. On January 4, 1919, Roosevelt's White House valet, James Amos, came to the Roosevelt household to help his former employer. Amos was concerned by what he found: the formerly robust man appeared weak and tired. The next night, Roosevelt complained of shortness of breath. An attending doctor gave him something to help him sleep. As James Amos helped him to bed, Roosevelt asked him to turn out the light. Those were his last words. Teddy Roosevelt died in his sleep of a coronary embolism.

The nation was shocked by his sudden death, and telegrams poured in from around the world. Both houses of Congress adjourned, and a forty-two-member delegation left for New York on a special train for the funeral. Former President William Howard Taft and Henry Cabot Lodge were among the other dignitaries who traveled to Oyster Bay.

As snow fell outside, a private service for the family was held at Sagamore Hill two days after Roosevelt's death. That afternoon, five hundred invited guests assembled at Christ Episcopal Church in Oyster Bay for a simple funeral service conducted by the Reverend George Talmage. Roosevelt's flag-draped oak coffin, topped by a wreath and two banners from his beloved Rough Riders cavalry, lay at the front of the church. When the service concluded, Roosevelt's body was taken by six pallbearers to Young's Memorial Cemetery for burial. An estimated four thousand people, including many schoolchildren, lined the procession route. At 2:59 p.m., as the casket was lowered into the ground, New York City observed a moment of silence in Roosevelt's honor.

Roosevelt selected his gravesite on a knoll overlooking the water. His grave is marked by a granite headstone bearing the presidential seal. Twenty-six steps lead to the grave, signifying Roosevelt's service as the nation's twenty-sixth president. A plaque on a nearby rock bears his own words: "Keep your eyes on the stars and keep your feet on the ground." Twenty-four other members of the Roosevelt family are buried in this section, among them his second wife Edith and two of his children.

Touring Theodore Roosevelt's Tomb at Young's Memorial Cemetery

Young's Memorial Cemetery is located in Oyster Bay, New York. It is open every day during daylight hours. Admission is free.

From New York City: Take the Long Island Expressway east to exit 41N. Turn left onto Route 106 and head north. Follow Route 106 to Oyster Bay. Turn right on East Main Street. Go two miles to Young's Memorial Cemetery, which is located on the right.

To find Theodore Roosevelt's grave, follow the signs on the cemetery walkway. Roosevelt's grave is located at the top of the staircase.

For additional information

Sagamore Hill National Historical Site
20 Sagamore Hill Road
Oyster Bay, New York 11771-1809
Phone: (516) 922-4788
Fax: (516) 922-4792
www.nps.gov/sahi

The "Rough Rider's" final resting place

Theodore Roosevelt

"Today TR lies near a Long Island bird sanctuary, a fitting end for the great conservationist who had ruffled congressional feathers…"

—Richard Norton Smith

On learning of the death of his youngest son, Quentin, shot down by German gunners in October 1918, Theodore Roosevelt had concealed his heartache behind characteristically belligerent prose. "Only those are fit to live who do not fear to die," he wrote defiantly, "and none are fit to die who have shrunk from the joy of life and the duty of life. Both life and death are part of the same Great Adventure."

On the night of January 5, 1919, an exhausted TR put down one of his ever-present volumes and remarked to his wife, Edith, "I wonder if you'll ever know how I love Sagamore Hill." Shortly afterward the old lion instructed his valet, "James, will you please put out the light?" They were his last words. Before dawn a blood clot stole into his lungs, carrying off the most lovable of presidents. Three thousand miles away, on a train streaking across the French countryside, Woodrow Wilson was informed of Roosevelt's death. Observant reporters noticed an expression of surprise on the president's face, soon replaced by something close to triumph. More gracious was Wilson's vice president, Thomas Marshall, who said of the fallen rival, "Death had to take him sleeping, for if Roosevelt had been awake, there would have been a fight."

Vetoing any Washington services, the Roosevelt family instead planned a simple ceremony, without music or eulogy, in a nearby Episcopal chapel. Arriving late, William Howard Taft was put in a pew with family servants before Roosevelt's son, Archie, spied him.

The Roosevelt family plot at Young's Memorial Cemetery

"You're a dear personal friend and you must come up further," the young man told Taft, who had more or less reconciled with Roosevelt following their bitter 1912 falling out. Afterwards, mourners made their way to a nearby hillside flecked with snow. Here Taft remained a long while as his friend's body was lowered into the ground. Some thought they saw tears streaming down his face. Perhaps; that night he attended a New York theater performance. Today TR lies near a Long Island bird sanctuary, a fitting end for the great conservationist who had ruffled congressional feathers by unilaterally preserving wetlands and other habitats filled with the creatures he had loved, and slaughtered, since childhood.

— RNS

Theodore Roosevelt

William Howard Taft

Buried: Arlington National Cemetery, Arlington, Virginia

Twenty-seventh President — 1909-1913

Born: September 15, 1857, in Cincinnati, Ohio

Died: March 8, 1930, in Washington, D.C.

Age at death: 72

Cause of death: Heart disease

Final words: Unknown

Admission to Arlington National
Cemetery: Free

William Howard Taft, our twenty-seventh president, is probably best remembered for two things: he was the only president to serve as Chief Justice and, at 6'2" and 332 lbs., he was our largest president—so large that he reportedly got stuck in a White House bathtub. An outsized tub was created specially for him.

He also had the distinction of having the first presidential funeral to be broadcast to the nation via radio.

Taft was not a particularly happy president. In 1912, Theodore Roosevelt challenged his former protégé for the Republican nomination. When that effort failed, Roosevelt waged a third-party challenge on the Bull Moose ticket, splitting the Republican vote. Defeated by Democrat Woodrow Wilson, Taft retired from the White House to a career in law.

William Howard Taft's granite monument

In 1921, President Harding appointed him Chief Justice of the Supreme Court.

Taft spent nine vigorous years on the court, stepping down in February 1930 when the strain of his excess weight began to seriously affect his health. Diagnosed with heart disease and high blood pressure, Taft failed quickly. By March, he was drifting in and out of consciousness. With his wife Nellie at his side, he died in his sleep at their home on March 8. Taft was seventy-two.

President Hoover paid a condolence call to Taft's widow at the couple's home on Wyoming Avenue in Washington, D.C., and issued a proclamation honoring him. For burial, Nellie dressed her husband in his black judicial robe. A military procession escorted the body from the Taft home, past the White House and to the Capitol. Taft's body lay in state while thousands of mourners waited in torrential downpours to pay their respects.

A memorial service for the ex-president was held at All Soul's Unitarian Church on Sixteenth Street in Washington; a six-horse caisson carried the body to the church while an army band played Chopin's funeral march. President and Mrs. Hoover were among the guests for the simple service with no eulogy. A string quartet and an organist played hymns and the Reverend Ulysses Grant Pierce read some of Taft's favorite poems, including Wordsworth's "Character of the Happy Warrior." A radio microphone hidden among the flowers broadcast the tribute to listeners across the country.

Taft's funeral procession was as outsized as he. A hearse carried Taft's flag-draped coffin to Arlington National Cemetery escorted by 120 cars. A large truck carried hundreds of flower arrangements. A thousand soldiers presented arms before a bugler sounded taps. A minister read the 23rd Psalm. Taft was laid to rest among white oak and chestnut trees, one of only two presidents (John Kennedy is the other) buried at Arlington. Nellie, the first lady responsible for Washington's famed cherry trees, was buried alongside him when she died in 1943.

Touring William Howard Taft's Tomb at Arlington National Cemetery

Arlington National Cemetery is open daily, 365 days a year. Hours are from 8:00 a.m. to 7:00 p.m. from April through September and 8:00 a.m. to 5:00 p.m. from October through March. Admission to the cemetery is free.

Arlington National Cemetery is located across the Potomac River from Washington, D.C., at the north end of the Memorial Bridge. The bridge is accessible from Constitution Avenue or Twenty-third Street N.W. near the Lincoln Memorial. The cemetery can also be reached by Metrorail, at the Arlington Cemetery stop on the blue line.

Cars are not allowed on the cemetery grounds except by special permission. There is ample paid parking available near the Visitors Center. Motorized tours of the cemetery are available for a fee through Tourmobile; however, the Taft gravesite is not one of the tour's scheduled stops.

Maps of the cemetery are available at the Visitors Center. To reach Taft's grave from the cemetery's main entrance (Memorial Drive), go right onto Schley Drive. Brown signs lead the way to the Taft gravesite.

For additional information

Superintendent
Arlington National Cemetery
Arlington, VA 22211
Visitor Center Phone:
(703) 607-8000
www.arlingtoncemetery.org

The Taft gravesite at Arlington National Cemetery

"Taft made up in principle what he lacked in political dexterity. " —*Richard Norton Smith*

William Howard Taft and John F. Kennedy might seem, at first glance, a presidential odd couple. In truth, they share more than a common resting place. Long before he became the first American president to be buried at Arlington National Cemetery, Taft was the victim of religious bias. During the 1908 campaign, a Presbyterian minister in his native Cincinnati urged his flock to vote for Taft's opponent, William Jennings Bryan. The man of the cloth accused Taft of being overly friendly to Roman Catholics, with whom he had negotiated a landmark sale of church properties as governor general of the Philippines.

A more serious controversy involved Taft's less than orthodox beliefs. "I am a Unitarian," he wrote forthrightly. "I believe in God. I do not believe in the Divinity of Christ." Under the circumstances, Taft had felt it necessary to withdraw his name from consideration for the Yale presidency. The White House was a different story.

A maladroit politician, Taft made things worse by playing golf on Sundays. Theodore Roosevelt advised him to be more discreet. Moreover, said TR, golf was viewed in many quarters as an elite pastime. Taft was confused. His friend the president played tennis—if anything a more rarified game. True enough, replied Roosevelt. But there was a difference: he didn't allow photographers to take his picture.

Taft made up in principle what he lacked in political dexterity. "Of course, I'm interested in the spread of Christian civilization," he wrote to one concerned voter in August 1908, "but to go into a dogmatic discussion of creed I will not do whether I am defeated or not...if the American electorate is so narrow as not to want a Unitarian, well and good. I can stand it."

— RNS

William Howard Taft

Woodrow Wilson

Buried: Washington National Cathedral, Washington, D.C.

Twenty-eighth President — 1913-1921

Born: December 28, 1856, in Staunton, Virginia

Died: 11:15 a.m. on February 3, 1924, in Washington, D.C.

Age at death: 67

Cause of death: Heart failure

Final words: "The machinery is worn out. I am ready.... Edith!..."

Admission to Washington National Cathedral: Free

The only president with a Ph.D. (in political science), Woodrow Wilson earned a Nobel Peace Prize for his role in ending World War I and creating the League of Nations. His administration also saw the addition of three amendments to the Constitution: the seventeenth, for direct election of U.S. Senators; the eighteenth, prohibiting the sale of alcohol; and the nineteenth, granting women the right to vote.

Wilson was a college professor and president of Princeton University before he entered the political arena. In his first attempt at public office, Wilson won the governorship of New Jersey in 1910. He had barely taken over the job when his name was thrown into the ring for the 1912 Democratic presidential nomination. A compelling speaker, he emerged from a fractious convention and went on to defeat William Howard Taft and

Woodrow Wilson was laid to rest in the nave of Washington National Cathedral

Bull Moose candidate Theodore Roosevelt to win the White House. On a cold day in March 1913, Wilson took the oath of office with his wife Ellen at his side.

Ellen would serve just a short time as first lady. She died in 1914 as the "guns of August" signaled the start of World War I. The president was so distraught that his depression lifted only after he met and married Edith Bolling Galt the following year. His physical health had begun to decline, largely due to overwork. He was consumed with efforts to keep the United States out of the growing world war.

Wilson suffered his first small stroke in 1906, which left him blind in one eye. He was plagued by headaches and high blood pressure, occasionally employing a stomach pump to relieve chronic stomach ailments. In 1919 while traveling to build public support for the Treaty of Versailles, Wilson suffered a more serious stroke. This one left him paralyzed on one side and barely able to speak.

Eventually Wilson was able to walk with a cane, but his health was so precarious that Mrs. Wilson began running interference for her husband. By her own account, she reviewed papers and meeting requests to decide which ones were important enough to go the president. Thus Edith Wilson became known as the "Secret President" and the "first woman to run the government."

When he retired in 1921 after serving two terms, Wilson rarely left his home on S Street in Washington. One of his last public appearances was at Warren Harding's funeral in August 1923. In the last weeks of his life,

Wilson was virtually blind, barely able to move or speak. Edith Wilson, still working at her husband's side, knew the end was near.

On February 1, 1924, Wilson, lying on his large canopied bed, spoke his last sentences before losing consciousness: "The machinery is worn out. I am ready." Reporters and curiosity seekers gathered outside the home, waiting for bulletins from the dying man's doctors. Wilson regained consciousness just long enough to call out for his wife. On February 3, his heart stopped beating. His wife and daughter Margaret were at his side.

Five days later, thirty thousand people braved rain, snow, and bitter cold to line the funeral route. A small private service, attended by President and Mrs. Coolidge, was held in the music room of the house on S Street. Ministers read the 23rd Psalm while a grief stricken Edith Wilson watched the proceedings from the top of the stairs.

Atop the closed black casket lay a spray of orchids from the dead man's widow. Wilson's body was borne across the city by a military escort to the unfinished Washington National Cathedral for an Episcopal funeral service that was broadcast on the radio. The organist, who had also served as Wilson's confidential stenographer for thirteen years, played some of his favorite hymns.

After all of the guests departed, Wilson's casket was lowered into a crypt; it was later moved to the nave. Edith Wilson remained at their home on S Street until her death in 1961. She is buried next to her husband at the National Cathedral.

Touring Woodrow Wilson's Tomb at Washington National Cathedral

Washington National Cathedral is located at the intersection of Massachusetts and Wisconsin Avenues in Washington, D.C. Free parking is available but limited on the north and south sides of the Cathedral grounds. The Cathedral is open Monday through Friday from 10:00 a.m. to 5:30 p.m., Saturday from 10:00 a.m. to 4:30 p.m., and Sunday from 8:00 a.m. to 5:30 p.m. The nave level, where Wilson's tomb is located, remains open until 9:00 p.m. from May 1 through Labor Day. The nave is often closed on Saturdays throughout the year for special events. Admission is free.

From downtown Washington: Take Massachusetts Avenue north and follow to Wisconsin Avenue. Turn right onto Wisconsin Avenue. The Cathedral will be on your immediate right.

From Maryland and the north: Take I-95 to I-495 West, the Capital Beltway. Exit south on Wisconsin Avenue. The Cathedral is approximately 6.5 miles ahead on the left.

From Virginia and the south: Take I-495 over the American Legion Bridge into Maryland and take the Wisconsin Avenue/Bethesda exit. The Cathedral is approximately 6.5 miles on the left. Or, take the Memorial Bridge to the Lincoln Memorial, bearing right onto Rock Creek Parkway. (Note: Rock Creek Parkway is one way southbound during morning rush hour; buses cannot exit on Massachusetts Avenue.) Follow the parkway to Massachusetts Avenue, turning left onto Massachusetts Avenue. Follow Massachusetts Avenue to Wisconsin Avenue, and turn right. The Cathedral is on the immediate right.

The Cathedral is also accessible via Metrorail and Metrobus. On Metrorail, take the red line to the Tenleytown/AU station. Be sure to get a free bus transfer at the station. Exit on the west side of Wisconsin Avenue. Take any "30" series bus (#31, #32, #36, or #37) going south on Wisconsin Avenue. Ride approximately one and a half miles south on Wisconsin Avenue to the Cathedral.

To find Wilson's tomb once inside the Cathedral, look for the Woodrow Wilson Bay at the center of the nave on the south side.

For additional information

Washington National Cathedral
Massachusetts and Wisconsin Avenues, NW
Washington, D.C. 20016-5098
Phone: (202) 537-6200
Fax: (202) 364-6600
www.cathedral.org/cathedral

"…an ailing Wilson insisted there would be no American entry into the League of Nations except on his terms." —Richard Norton Smith

If Theodore Roosevelt died too soon, Woodrow Wilson may have lived too long, in the process recalling Oscar Wilde's lament that "each man kills the thing he loves." Following a stroke in October 1919, an ailing Wilson insisted there would be no American entry into the League of Nations except on his terms.

In February 1924 when the ex-president "went west"—to use the euphemism popularized by World War I soldiers—he was buried under the floor of Bethlehem Chapel in Washington's uncompleted Cathedral of Saints Peter and Paul. Despite the presence of Admiral George Dewey, Cordell Hall, and Helen Keller, the National Cathedral never realized its planners' original intent as a kind of American Westminister Abbey. But it attracts thousands of pilgrims each year, many of whom pause in the cool stone bay off the main nave where today the preacher's son from Staunton, Virginia rests beneath a crusader's cross.

— RNS

Wilson's second wife, Edith, survived him by thirty-seven years. She is buried with him at the Cathedral.

Warren G. Harding

Buried: Harding Tomb, Marion, Ohio

Twenty-ninth President – 1921-1923

Born: November 2, 1865, in Corsica, Ohio

Died: 7:30 p.m. on August 2, 1923, in San Francisco, California

Age at death: 57

Cause of death: Heart attack

Final words: "That's good. Go on, read some more."

Admission to Harding Tomb: Free

Warren Harding's administration lasted just over two years. His election to the presidency was the first in which women were allowed to vote nationwide. He was also the first president to ride in a car to his inauguration. A popular chief executive, he and his wife Florence hosted frequent parties at the White House, complete with alcohol then forbidden by the eighteenth amendment.

The couple was on a tour of the western states in the summer of 1923 when the president, already suffering from exhaustion, fell ill. Mrs. Harding stayed at his bedside in San Francisco's Palace Hotel. She read him an article from the *Saturday Evening Post* that portrayed him in a favorable light. President Harding, deeply concerned over several brewing scandals involving members of his administration, must have been surprised. Pleased to hear some good publicity, he asked her to read on. It was his last request. Moments later, he died of a heart attack.

The president's doctor first suspected food poisoning. Others blamed "apoplexy," the term then used to describe a stroke. One journalist even accused Florence Harding of poisoning her husband as punishment for his extramarital affairs. Nothing sinister was ever proven.

Vice President Calvin Coolidge was vacationing at his father's home in Plymouth Notch, Vermont, when he got the news in the middle of the night. Coolidge's father, a notary public, swore in his son as the thirtieth president of the United States in the sitting room of the family home.

The nation was stunned. Special edition newspapers were snatched up while the ink was still wet. Thousands turned out to see the funeral train that brought Harding's body back to the East Room of the White House. Public mourning continued at the Capitol, where thirty thousand citizens passed by his coffin, resting on the same catafalque used for Abraham Lincoln.

The third president from Ohio to die in office was taken back to his father's home in Marion, Ohio. Nearly all of the town's residents paid their respects. Harding's body was placed in a temporary vault at Marion

School children donated their pennies to fund construction of the Harding Memorial

Warren and Florence Harding are buried together at the Harding Tomb

Cemetery while public funds were raised to construct a monument in his honor. His wife lived just one year more.

In 1927, the bodies of Warren and Florence Harding were moved to the newly constructed Harding Memorial. It was dedicated in 1931 by President Herbert Hoover.

Touring Warren G. Harding's Tomb at the Harding Memorial

The Harding Memorial is located in a ten-acre landscaped park in Marion, Ohio, on State Route 423. The Harding Tomb is at the corner of State Route 423 and Vernon Heights Boulevard in Marion. Vernon Heights is about 1.5 miles west of U.S. Route 23 off of State Route 95 in Marion County.

The Harding Tomb is open year-round during daylight hours. Admission is free.

For additional information

Harding Tomb
Vernon Heights Boulevard
Marion, OH 43302
Phone: (740) 387-9630
www.ohiohistory.org/places/hardtomb

"Unfortunately, he received the worst possible treatment from a quack named Charles Sawyer…" —*Richard Norton Smith*

On June 20, 1923, Harding and his party of sixty-five left Washington's Union Station for what the beleaguered president called a "Voyage of Understanding." Traveling through the isolationist Midwest, Harding showed genuine courage in advocating U.S. membership in the World Court. "I want America to play her part in helping to abolish war," he told an audience in Salt Lake City.

But the trip had a somber subtext, one invisible to the large and enthusiastic crowds that turned out to greet the popular chief executive. Secretary of Commerce Herbert Hoover never forgot the round-the-clock bridge games with which the president distracted himself.

"If you knew of a great scandal in our administration," Harding asked Hoover, "would you for the good of the country and the party expose it publicly or would you bury it?"

"Publish it," said Hoover, "and at least get credit for integrity on your side."

Pressing for details, Hoover heard vague talk of "irregularities" in the Justice Department, where a close associate of Attorney General Henry Daugherty had recently committed suicide. As the grueling trip proceeded, Harding's health visibly deteriorated. Unfortunately, he received the worst possible treatment from a quack named Charles Sawyer, an old Marion acquaintance favored by the First Lady. It was "Doc" Sawyer, for example, who blamed the president's collapse in Alaska on some tainted crabmeat.

By the time he arrived in San Francisco on July 29, Harding was at death's door, his enlarged heart,

Marion, Ohio

The Harding Tomb, one of five presidential gravesites in Ohio, contains exhibits detailing Harding's life

already taxed by pneumonia, put under intolerable strain by a deadly combination of stimulants and purgatives prescribed by Doc Sawyer.

August 2, a sultry Thursday in the nation's capital. A few minutes after 10 p.m., Mrs. Harding's favorite astrologer, a former vaudevillian and Coney Island palm reader reborn as Madame Marsha, held court in a Dupont Circle townhouse. Asked by newspapermen about reports that Harding was suffering from food poisoning, Madame Marsha quietly replied, "The president is dead."

And so he was, having succumbed to a massive coronary a few minutes earlier in his San Francisco hotel room. Returning to the White House, Florence Harding sat by her husband's open casket for a post-midnight monologue with the rouged corpse. "No one can hurt you now, Warren," she told him, thereby putting the seal on the creepiest administration in American history.

— RNS

Calvin Coolidge

Buried: Plymouth Cemetery, Plymouth, Vermont

Thirtieth President – 1923-1929

Born: July 4, 1872, in Plymouth, Vermont

Died: 12:45 p.m. on January 5, 1933, in Northampton, Massachusetts

Age at death: 60

Cause of death: Heart failure

Final words: Unknown

Admission to Plymouth Cemetery: Free

The classic illustration of "Silent Cal" Coolidge's personality involved a woman who bet she could make him say more than two words. He responded simply, "You lose."

The shy, frugal Coolidge married his perfect match: vivacious, outgoing Grace Goodhue. The two settled in Northampton, Massachusetts, where he began a career in public service that spanned three decades. He worked his way up through Republican ranks in his home state until he was elected governor in 1918. Coolidge's handling of a Boston police strike brought him national attention, earning him the vice presidential nomination in 1920.

Calvin Coolidge spent just two years as Warren Harding's vice president. When the president died on August 2, 1923, the vacationing Coolidge was roused from his bed at his

"Silent Cal" Coolidge's simple headstone

father's Vermont home to take the oath of office. His father, a notary public, swore in his son with a form he found on the shelves of his library.

The new president returned to Washington and tried to make the transition as smooth as possible. Grace Coolidge became a popular White House hostess. A healthy economy helped him win election in his own right the following year. Despite prosperity and political success, 1924 was a tragic year for the Coolidges. While playing tennis, sixteen-year-old Calvin Coolidge, Jr. got a blister on his toe that caused a fatal blood infection. His parents never got over their grief.

The couple sought privacy at their Northampton estate, The Beeches, after Coolidge's retirement in 1929. The former president wrote his autobiography and a daily newspaper column. On January 5, 1933, Grace Coolidge returned from a shopping trip to find her beloved husband dead of a heart attack.

Calvin Coolidge's funeral reflected his simple tastes in life. Funeral services were held at the Edwards Congregational Church in Northampton. Mourners, including President Herbert Hoover and Eleanor Roosevelt, paid their respects. Finally, his widow made a hundred mile trip by car to see the former president returned to his Vermont roots. He was buried on a steep hillside in the Coolidge family plot after a five-minute ceremony. Grace Coolidge was buried at his side when she died in 1957.

Each year on the Fourth of July, a wreath is laid at his grave in honor of the only president born on Independence Day.

Touring Calvin Coolidge's Tomb at Plymouth Cemetery

Plymouth Cemetery is open daily from dawn until dusk. Six generations of Coolidges are buried there. Admission is free.

From New York and New Jersey: Take I-87 through Albany to the Northway. Continue north on I-87 to exit 20/Fort Ann and Whitehall. Follow Route 149 East into Fort Ann. Turn left onto Route 4 and follow through Whitehall, New York and Rutland, Vermont.

From Rutland, Vermont: Make a right turn onto Route 7 South; travel approximately three miles and turn left onto Route 103. Go sixteen miles, then turn left onto Route 100 North. Travel approximately nine miles to Plymouth, and turn right onto Route 100A. Travel one mile and you will see a sign for the Calvin Coolidge Historic Site on the left.

From Long Island, Connecticut and Western Massachusetts: Take I-95 North to I-91 North to exit 6 at Rockingham, Vermont. Travel north on Route 103 through Chester and Ludlow to Route 100 North. Proceed north on Route 100 for approximately nine miles to Plymouth, then turn right onto Route 100A. Travel one mile and you will see a sign for the Calvin Coolidge Historic Site on the left.

From Boston and Rhode Island: From the Boston area, take I-93 North to Concord, New Hampshire. Just south of Concord take I-89 North to exit 1 in Vermont/Route 4 West for Woodstock–Rutland. Follow Route 4 to Route 100A, approximately eighteen miles. At Bridgewater Corners, turn left and follow 100A for approximately eight miles. You will see a sign for the Calvin Coolidge Historic Site on the right.

Once inside the cemetery, follow signs to President Coolidge's gravesite.

For additional information

President Calvin Coolidge State Historic Site
P.O. Box 247
Plymouth, Vermont 05056
Phone: (802) 672-3773
Fax: (802) 672-3337
www.historicvermont.org/coolidge

"…the recently opened papers of White House physician Joel Boone reveal just how great a toll the presidency exacted on Coolidge…"

—Richard Norton Smith

Nothing in his subsequent behavior was so revealing as Coolidge's conduct on that sultry night in August 1923, when Warren Harding died in a San Francisco hotel room and the new president was sworn into office by his seventy-two-year-old father, a Vermont notary public. Before setting out for Washington the next morning, Coolidge, a deeply sentimental man, visited the hillside cemetery where five generations of his family lay buried. He paused before the grave of his mother. Hers was the first picture he placed on his White House desk; he would carry her likeness with him until the day of his own death.

Exploding the myth of a do-nothing president who slept away his term, the recently opened papers of White House physician Joel Boone reveal just how great a toll the presidency exacted on Coolidge, who never recovered from the 1924 death of his namesake son. As he wrote in his spare yet revealing autobiography, when young Calvin died, he took the glory and the

Plymouth Cemetery is part of the Calvin Coolidge State Historic Site

Calvin Coolidge

Six generations of the Coolidge family are buried on this Vermont hillside

power of the presidency with him. "The ways of Providence are often beyond our understanding," Coolidge added, in a Job-like cry of despair. "I do not know why such a price was exacted for occupying the White House."

Informed that ex-president Coolidge was dead in January 1933, Dorothy Parker famously wisecracked, "How can you tell?" H.L. Mencken responded differently. With the perspective of time, Mencken had come to reconsider his scathing criticism of the Coolidge presidency. Contrasting Coolidge with Wilson "the World Saver" and Hoover "the Wonder Boy," Mencken anticipated the revisionist scholarship of post-Reagan America. Should the day ever dawn, said the Sage of Baltimore, "when Jefferson's warnings are heeded at last, and we reduce government to its simplest terms, it may very well happen that Cal's bones now resting inconspicuously in the Vermont granite will come to be revered as those of a man who really did the nation some service."

Not a bad epitaph for one whose first thought on being roused from bed in the middle of the night and thrust into the presidency was "I believe I can swing it."

— RNS

Plymouth, Vermont

Herbert Hoover

Thirty-first President – 1929-1933
Born: August 10, 1874, in West Branch, Iowa
Died: October 20, 1964, in New York, New York
Age at death: 90
Cause of death: Bleeding from upper gastrointestinal tract; strained vascular system
Final words: Unknown
Admission to Herbert Hoover Library and Museum: $6.00

Though many associate his name with the bread lines of the Great Depression, Herbert Hoover was also responsible for feeding millions in Europe as part of the relief efforts during World War I. Hoover gained worldwide attention for his management of American aid programs that led to his appointment as Warren Harding's secretary of commerce in 1921. He was groomed unsuccessfully for the Republican vice presidential nomination in 1924, only to capture the top spot four years later.

In 1894 while studying geology at Stanford University, Hoover fell in love with Lou Henry, the only female student in the geology department. The two married on California's Pacific Coast on February 10, 1899. He earned his millions as a mining engineer before entering politics. The couple entertained lavishly during their years in the White House but did it all with their own funds. Hoover never accepted a salary for his service as president.

The stock market crashed in the first year of Hoover's administration. Unemployment continued to rise. Americans looking for a change elected Franklin Roosevelt to the presidency in 1932. Herbert Hoover attended Roosevelt's inauguration and retreated to his home in California. He later settled in New York City where he became a vocal critic of his successor's administration.

When war raged in Europe, Hoover returned to his earlier role as a relief organizer. During the Truman administration, he served as chairman of a commission that studied the effectiveness of the executive branch.

Entering his tenth decade, Hoover's rapidly declining health left him nearly deaf and blind. He spent his last days in a suite on the thirty-first floor of the Waldorf Towers in New York City. On October 19, 1964, Hoover slipped into a coma. He died the next morning of massive internal bleeding at age ninety.

The former president's closed coffin lay on public view for two days at Saint Bartholomew's Episcopal Church in New York City. There was also a brief private memorial service. Both of the candidates in that year's presidential race, Lyndon Johnson and Barry Goldwater, paid their respects. Former presidents Truman and Eisenhower were ill and unable to attend.

Herbert Hoover's boyhood home. His grave lies across the lawn to the left.

Hoover's body was taken to Washington by train where it lay in state in the Capitol Rotunda. President Johnson placed a wreath of red and white carnations before the funeral bier. The formal state occasion included a military guard and twenty-one-gun salute. Hoover's casket rested on the same catafalque used for John F. Kennedy's funeral the year before. The Senate chaplain, Frederick Brown Harris, remembered that "we bear the worn bodily tenement of the oldest chief executive to this highest pedestal of honor where so recently lay the martyred form of the youngest." He had it slightly wrong: Herbert Hoover was then our second-oldest former president. John Adams was 176 days older when he died. (And Gerald Ford passed them both, living to be 93 years, 165 days old.)

This museum display shows Hoover fly fishing, a favorite pastime

Hoover was buried in West Branch, Iowa according to his Quaker tradition. He had chosen the site himself, on a hill overlooking the two-room cottage where he was born. The simple graveside service was attended by seventy-five thousand mourners, some of whom had flown from Washington. Fifteen limousines carried the official delegation some thirty-three miles from the airport in Cedar Rapids. As the sun shone, Hoover's coffin was lowered into the ground to the sounds of the "Battle Hymn of the Republic." At the family's request, there was no gun salute.

Lou Hoover, who preceded her husband in death by twenty years, had been buried at their alma mater. Her body was re-interred with her husband's one month after his death.

Herbert Hoover

The Hoover Library and Museum is located near his birthplace in West Branch, Iowa

Touring the Tomb at the Herbert Hoover National Historic Site

The Herbert Hoover National Historic Site is located in West Branch, Iowa, ten miles east of Iowa City and offers guided tours for the summer season. It is open daily from 9:00 a.m. to 5:00 p.m., except Thanksgiving, Christmas, and New Year's Day. Admission to the historic site, including the birthplace and gravesite, is free. Admission to the Herbert Hoover Presidential Library and Museum is $6.00 for adults and $3.00 for senior citizens. Children sixteen and under are admitted free.

From the east or west: Take I-80 to exit 254. Travel 0.4 miles north to the Visitors Center. Maps to the gravesite are available at the Visitors Center.

To reach the gravesite from the Hoover National Historic Site on Main Street, turn south on Parkside Drive. Follow Parkside Drive until reaching Library Road. Turn right on Library Road heading west. Follow the signs to President Hoover's gravesite. Public parking is available near the gravesite.

To reach the grave on foot from the Historic Site, take the walkway from the Visitors Center to the Library Museum. Then follow signs to President Hoover's gravesite.

For additional information

Herbert Hoover National Historic Site
110 Parkside Drive
P.O. Box 607
West Branch, IA 52358
Phone: (319) 643-2541
Fax: (319) 643-7864
www.nps.gov/heho

ABOVE: Legendary bank robber John Dillinger is one of Benjamin Harrison's neighbors in Crown Hill Cemetery. Harrison's monument is the rectangular structure to the right of the tree at center. Crown Hill, the third largest non-government cemetery in the U.S., overlooks Indianapolis, Indiana.

PREVIOUS PAGE: Grover Cleveland's tomb in New Jersey's Princeton Cemetery. A neighboring epitaph reads, "I told you I was sick."

The McKinley Monument, located an hour south of Cleveland in Canton, Ohio played host to the C-SPAN School Bus in November 1993.

ABOVE: William Howard Taft (along with John F. Kennedy) is one of two presidents buried in Arlington National Cemetery. Another president's son, Robert Todd Lincoln, is buried nearby with his wife and son Abraham Lincoln II.

OPPOSITE PAGE: Teddy Roosevelt selected this gravesite on a knoll overlooking Oyster Bay on Long Island, about an hour's drive from New York City. The presidential seal is etched on his tombstone.

ABOVE: The twenty-ninth president is memorialized at the Harding Tomb in Marion, Ohio, an hour north of Columbus.

OPPOSITE: Washington National Cathedral was intended to be America's version of Westminister Abbey, a final resting place for national heroes. Woodrow Wilson is the only president buried here. Helen Keller and her teacher, Anne Sullivan Macy, are interred in the Cathedral's columbarium.

FOLLOWING PAGE: Our thirtieth president, Calvin Coolidge, is buried alongside his wife and son on a hillside near his boyhood home in Plymouth, Vermont.

"'I outlived the bastards,' [Hoover] said."

—Richard Norton Smith

The white marble gravestones of Herbert and Lou Hoover

Asked in the twilight of life how he managed to survive the long years of ostracism coinciding with the New Deal, Hoover gave a characteristically pungent response. "I outlived the bastards," he said.

But not even Hoover could outrace the rigors of old age. In October 1964, he learned of a domestic accident involving one of his closest, if most unlikely, friends. "Bathtubs are a menace to ex-presidents," he informed Harry Truman. "For as you may recall, a bathtub rose up and fractured my vertebrae when I was in Venezuela on your world famine mission in 1946." It was the last communication sent from Hoover's Waldorf Towers suite.

His death six days later at age 90 evoked twinges of guilt as well as grief. While he might be remembered by many as "the Great Objector," columnist Walter Lippmann wrote, "that was the tragic result of having been run over by the Great Depression." Such negativism was not in harmony with Hoover's "generous, liberal and magnanimous nature." In common with the crowds who assembled in New York, Washington, and Iowa to bid farewell to the nation's thirty-first president, Lippmann preferred to remember Hoover as "a bold and brilliant philanthropist who binds up wounds and avoids inflicting them."

— RNS

Herbert Hoover

Franklin Delano Roosevelt

Buried: Franklin D. Roosevelt Library and Museum, Hyde Park, New York

Thirty-second President – 1933-1945

Born: January 30, 1882, in Hyde Park, New York

Died: April 12, 1945, in Warm Springs, Georgia

Age at death: 63

Cause of death: Cerebral hemorrhage

Final words: "I have a terrific headache."

Admission to Franklin Roosevelt Library and Museum: $14.00

Franklin Delano Roosevelt, master of the fireside chat, was the only president elected to four terms. He was at the nation's helm during two major events of the twentieth century: the Great Depression and World War II. Governor of New York when he won the Democratic presidential nomination in 1932, Roosevelt spoke of a "New Deal" for the American people, which became a hallmark of his administration.

In addition to the economic crisis at home, events overseas occupied much of the president's attention. On December 8, 1941, FDR asked Congress to declare war on Japan after the bombing of Hawaii's Pearl Harbor. Soon thereafter, the United States enjoined the Allies in Europe. The war lasted through the remainder of Roosevelt's service as president.

Franklin Roosevelt was a cousin of our twenty-sixth president, Theodore Roosevelt. He was also a distant relative

Franklin Delano Roosevelt's Hyde Park home

of two other U.S. presidents (Ulysses S. Grant and Zachary Taylor) and of British Prime Minister Winston Churchill. FDR married yet another distant cousin: Anna Eleanor Roosevelt, his fifth cousin once removed. Eleanor Roosevelt became an activist first lady, holding regular press conferences and speaking out on social issues.

During his third term in the White House, Franklin Roosevelt grew increasingly fatigued. He'd been stricken with polio at age thirty-nine which left his lower body paralyzed. Though unable to walk without crutches, his energy had always seemed boundless. But by March 1945, Roosevelt felt the need to retreat to Warm Springs, Georgia—a spot dubbed the "Little White House"—for some much-needed rest.

Surrounded by friends, including his onetime mistress, Lucy Mercer Rutherfurd, Roosevelt soon seemed like his old self again. The group went for leisurely drives in the country by day and spent their evenings with long meals and conversation. On the morning of April 12, his guests thought FDR looked better than he had in weeks. Lucy Rutherfurd's friend, Elizabeth Shoumatoff, was sketching the president's portrait when he raised his hand and said, "I have a terrific headache."

Franklin Delano Roosevelt

Those were his last words. FDR fell unconscious. He was carried to his bedroom by his valet and butler. The doctor came almost immediately, but nothing could be done. The president had suffered a massive brain injury. He died just before 3:30 that afternoon without regaining consciousness. For propriety's sake, Lucy Rutherfurd and Elizabeth Shoumatoff made a hasty departure from the "Little White House."

The First Lady was summoned back to the White House from a charity event she was attending. When she arrived, Press Secretary Steve Early and Dr. Ross McIntire told her that the president was dead. Soon after, Eleanor Roosevelt broke the news to Harry Truman that he was president.

At 7:00 p.m. that evening in Washington, D.C., Harry Truman took the oath of office. A few minutes later, Mrs. Roosevelt flew to Warm Springs. The next morning, Eleanor began the 800-mile trip back to Washington on the presidential train, her husband's bronze coffin visible through the windows. Hundreds of thousands lined the route, crying and praying. When the train pulled into Union Station, a military procession escorted the late president's body back to the White House. There, Eleanor was alone with her husband for the last time, placing her gold ring on his finger.

A simple funeral service was held in the East Room. The Roosevelt family was joined by the new president and his family, government leaders and heads of state. Mrs. Roosevelt remained stoic while others wept. Hymns were sung, including "Faith of Our Fathers," the president's favorite. The service ended with the famous line from FDR's first inaugural: "The only thing we have to fear is fear itself."

Before his death, Franklin Roosevelt indicated his wish to be buried at the family estate in Hyde Park, New York. His body was borne home for the last time on the presidential train. On arrival, the casket was placed on a caisson drawn by six horses, led by a riderless horse. The cortege was met at the gravesite by President Truman, the cabinet, numerous dignitaries, family, and friends. A military band played. Cannons were fired. A gun salute sounded. The longest-serving president was laid to rest beneath a monument listing only the dates of his birth and death.

Eleanor Roosevelt continued to lead an active life for nearly twenty years. She died of tuberculosis in 1962 and is buried next to her husband in Hyde Park. Franklin Roosevelt's beloved Scottish terrier, "Fala," is also buried near his master.

Hyde Park, New York

Touring the Tomb at the Franklin D. Roosevelt Library and Museum in Hyde Park, New York

The Franklin D. Roosevelt Library and Museum is open daily from 9:00 a.m. to 5:00 p.m., except New Year's Day, Thanksgiving, and Christmas. April through October, the site remains open until 6:00 p.m. Hours are subject to change and visitors are advised to call for further information. Self-guided tours of the museum and FDR home are available. There is a $14.00 admission fee for visitors sixteen years and older. Children fifteen and under are admitted free. Tours of the museum are $7.00, and tours of the home are an additional $7.00. A combination admission ticket to both the museum and the home of Franklin D. Roosevelt is $14.00. To visit the home with a group of ten or more, you must make a reservation by calling (800) 967–2283. The grounds and burial site are free and open from dawn to dusk.

From Manhattan/Albany/New Jersey: Take the New York State Thruway to exit 18 at New Paltz. Follow Route 299 East to Route 9W South. Cross the Mid-Hudson Bridge to Route 9 North. The Library is on the left, four miles north of Poughkeepsie.

From Long Island: Take the Long Island Expressway to the Cross Island Parkway. Cross the Whitestone Bridge. Follow the Hutchinson River Parkway to Route 684 North, then Route 84 West to Route 9 North. The library is on the left, four miles north of Poughkeepsie.

From Connecticut: Take Route 84 West to Route 9 North. The library is on the left side of Route 9, four miles north of Poughkeepsie.

To reach the tomb from the ticket booth, walk toward the west end of the parking lot leading into the site. Follow the signs to the FDR Rose Garden. The gravesite is located in the middle of the Rose Garden.

For additional information

The Museum of the Franklin D. Roosevelt Library
4079 Albany Post Road
Hyde Park, NY 12538
Phone: 1-800-FDR-VISIT or (845) 486-7770
Fax: (845) 486-1147
www.fdrlibrary.marist.edu

"In Berlin, Hitler's propaganda chief, Joseph Goebbels, called for champagne on learning of Roosevelt's death." —*Richard Norton Smith*

On the final morning of his life, surrounded by newspaper accounts of the steady advances being made by Allied armies in Europe and Asia, Franklin D. Roosevelt chatted with Lizzie McDuffie, a two-hundred-pound housekeeper who interrupted her dusting of the "Little White House" at Warm Springs to discuss theories of reincarnation. If there were such a thing, said Lizzie, she hoped to come back to life as a canary bird—an image whose very improbability caused FDR to roar with laughter. It was a perfect sendoff for the Happy Warrior of whom Churchill once said that meeting him was like opening a bottle of champagne.

In Berlin, Hitler's propaganda chief, Joseph Goebbels, called for champagne on learning of Roosevelt's death. In Moscow, Joseph Stalin asked Averell Harriman what the Soviet Union could do to show its

admiration for the late president. "Send Molotov to the San Francisco Conference," replied Harriman. The conference was called by Roosevelt to organize the postwar United Nations.

Stalin nodded. "The Foreign Minister will go."

At the New York Times an editorial writer composing a tribute for the next day's editions tapped out, "Men will thank God on their knees a hundred years from now, that Franklin D. Roosevelt was in the White House." At Warm Springs, an Atlanta mortician named Fred W. Patterson struggled to embalm the president's arteriosclerotic body. Patterson and his co-workers finally resorted to individual injections by hypodermic syringe.

Mrs. Roosevelt asked Grace Tully, FDR's secretary, if he had left instructions regarding his burial. As it turned out he had, but they would not be found until after the Hyde Park funeral. (The local selectmen had to

Hyde Park, New York

Franklin and Eleanor Roosevelt's gravesite. FDR's dog Fala is also buried there.

be tracked down at their homes, since a special permit was required to allow the president to be buried on his own estate.) According to Tully, Roosevelt had asked to be buried at sea in the event of his death while on the water. The sea had always seemed like home, he remarked.

Otherwise, FDR expressed his preference for a service "of utmost simplicity" in the East Room of the White House. No lying in state. A simple ceremony in the Capitol Rotunda, with two hymns and "no speaking." A funeral train to arrive in Hyde Park at 8:00 p.m., followed by a brief service at St. James Church "for old neighbors." A final evening in front of the fireplace of his mother's "Big Room." Burial the next morning in Sarah Roosevelt's rose garden, with the president's dark wood casket to be carried to the grave by workers on the nearby estates.

There was to be no public viewing—on that score Franklin and Eleanor were as one. Regarding his tombstone, FDR asked for an austere marker containing only the names and dates of his wife and himself. Thus Eleanor's wish to have inscribed the famous line "The only thing we have to fear is fear itself" on the marble block was overridden by her husband's preferences.

— RNS

Harry S. Truman

Buried: Harry S. Truman Library, Independence, Missouri

Thirty-third President – 1945-1953

Born: May 8, 1884, in Lamar, Missouri

Died: 7:50 a.m. on December 26, 1972, in Kansas City, Missouri

Age at death: 88

Cause of death: Cardiovascular failure

Final Words: Unknown

Admission to Harry S. Truman Library: $8.00

Harry Truman was having cocktails in the Capitol with House Speaker Sam Rayburn when FDR died and he became president on April 12, 1945. He later said, "I felt like the moon, the stars, and all the planets had fallen on me."

Eleanor Roosevelt met Truman at the White House to relay the news of her husband's death. When he asked if there was anything he could do, she responded, "No, Harry. Is there anything we can do for you? You're the one in trouble now." He had been vice president less than three months.

During "Give 'Em Hell Harry's" administration the atomic bomb was used against Japan, World War II ended, the Korean War began, and the United Nations was established. Truman also oversaw big changes at home—his home— during his presidency. The interior of the White House needed to be rebuilt after a piano leg fell through a crumbling floor. For four years, the Truman family lived across the street at Blair House.

Truman's wife Bess, his childhood sweetheart, found one advantage to being displaced: fewer social obligations. She disliked life as first lady and was thrilled when her husband decided not to seek a second full term.

In 1953, the couple returned to their home at 219 North Delaware in Independence, Missouri. Truman supervised the creation of his presidential library, which opened in 1957. He worked on his memoirs in an office there and loved to give tours to visitors surprised to see the former president on site.

By 1964, Truman was increasingly frail. After a fall in his home, the eighty-year-old former president never fully regained his strength. In early December 1972, Truman left his home for the last time and was admitted to Kansas City's Research Hospital. He was seriously ill with lung congestion and bronchitis. His condition improved briefly, but on December 14, Harry Truman lost consciousness. Most of his major organs were shutting down. By Christmas Eve, Truman was near death. His heart stopped at 7:50 a.m. on December 26, 1972. He was eighty-eight years old.

The government's plans for Truman's funeral were extensive. Arrangements by the Military District of Washington called for a five-day state affair, with his body being flown to Washington to lie in state in the Capitol Rotunda. The army even prepared "Black Jack," the riderless horse used in John Kennedy's funeral, for a flight to Missouri for the burial. However, Citizen Truman had himself vetoed the notion of lying in state. He and his wife opted instead for a simple private ceremony in Independence.

Still the streets were lined with soldiers on the day Truman took his final trip to his library. President and Mrs. Nixon laid a wreath of carnations on the casket. Lyndon Johnson, who was also there, would himself live just three more weeks.

An estimated seventy-five thousand people paid their respects before Truman was buried in the library's courtyard. As he'd told his staff, he wanted to be "out there, so I can get up and walk into my office if I want to." There was a simple graveside service with no hymns and no eulogy. He was laid to rest in the bitter cold to the sounds of taps. His beloved Bess was buried alongside him when she died in 1982 at age ninety-seven. She is America's longest-living first lady.

Touring the Tomb at the
Harry S. Truman Library

The Harry S. Truman Library and Museum is open daily, except Thanksgiving, Christmas, and New Year's Day. It is open from 9:00 a.m. to 5:00 p.m., Monday through Saturday, with extended hours until 9:00 p.m. on Thursdays from May through September. Sunday hours are from noon to 5:00 p.m.

Admission is $8.00 for adults, $7.00 for senior citizens, and $3.00 for children ages six to fifteen. Children under six are admitted free.

From Kansas City International Airport: Travel east/south on I-435 approximately thirty-two miles to the Winner Road exit. Winner Road becomes U.S. Highway 24. Travel east three miles to the library, which is on the north side of U.S. Highway 24.

From the north: Take I-35 to I-435 South to Winner Road/U.S. Highway 24 East. The library is on the north side of U.S. Highway 24.

From the east: Take I-70 to Noland Road north (about 5 miles) to U.S. Highway 24 West (about one mile). Look for the Harry S. Truman Library sign at the intersection of Noland Road and U.S. Highway 24.

From the south: Take I-35 to I-435 North to Winner Road/U.S. Highway 24 East. The library is on the north side of U.S. Highway 24.

From the west: Take I-70 to I-435 North, to Winner Road/U.S. Highway 24 East. The library is on the north side of U.S. Highway 24.

To reach the gravesite from the Library and Museum's east entrance, go to the courtyard. President Truman's grave is located in the center.

For additional information

Harry S. Truman Library
500 West U.S. Highway 24
Independence, MO 64050-1798
Phone: (800) 833-1225/(816) 268-8200
Fax: (816) 268-8295
www.trumanlibrary.org

"...funerals invite reconciliation."

—Richard Norton Smith

A man defines himself in many ways, not least of all through his loyalties. In January 1945, less than a week after being sworn in as Franklin Roosevelt's vice president, Harry Truman learned of the death of Tom Pendergast, the Kansas City politico who had sponsored Truman's early career and who had later gone to prison on charges of income tax evasion. Courageously, Truman decided to attend "the Big Boss's" funeral. It was a lifelong habit. In his magisterial *Truman*, David McCullough quotes an Independence minister who was taken aback one bleak winter day to find himself presiding over a committal service at which the sole mourner was the thirty-third President of the United States. Having said the benediction, the pastor turned to Truman.

"Mr. President, why are you here?" he asked. "It's cold and bitter. Did you know this gentleman?"

"Pastor," replied Truman, "I never forget a friend."

Old men spend an inordinate amount of time burying each other. At the same time, funerals invite

Truman's home at 219 North Delaware Street, a few blocks from his library

reconciliation. For example, it took the burial of John F. Kennedy to bring Truman together with his successor, Dwight Eisenhower, after a period of estrangement that dated back to the 1952 campaign. Truman never forgave Eisenhower for failing to come to the defense of General George Marshall when the former secretary of state

Harry S. Truman

was attacked by Joe McCarthy. For his part, Eisenhower resented Truman's strident attacks in the closing days of the campaign (in later years, he acidly dismissed New York's patrician governor, Averell Harriman, as "a Park Avenue Truman").

Yet when Marshall died in the fall of 1959, the two men sat side by side in the Fort Myer chapel where Marshall was memorialized. Two years later they attended the funeral of Speaker Sam Rayburn. Joined by President Kennedy and Vice President Lyndon Johnson, they were on hand in the rose garden at Hyde Park as Eleanor Roosevelt was laid to rest in November 1962. But it was the Kennedy funeral, during which they rode together to and from the services at Arlington, that drained the poison from their relationship. After the services, Truman and Eisenhower spent an hour reminiscing at Blair House, being careful to avoid past controversies.

— RNS

Dwight D. Eisenhower

Buried: Dwight D. Eisenhower Library and Museum, Abilene, Kansas

Thirty-fourth President – 1953-1961

Born: October 14, 1890, in Denison, Texas

Died: 12:35 p.m. on March 28, 1969, in Washington, D.C.

Age at death: 78

Cause of death: Congestive heart failure

Last words: "I want to go. God take me."

Admission to Dwight D. Eisenhower Library and Museum: $8.00

Dwight Eisenhower's childhood fascination with military history led him to West Point. He worked his way up through the army ranks to become a five-star general—one of only five in history. A hero of World War II, Eisenhower held the lofty title of Supreme Commander of the North Atlantic Treaty Organization when he won the Republican presidential nomination in 1952. In both the '52 and '56 elections he ran successfully against Democrat Adlai Stevenson.

In his two terms as president, the lifelong military man saw the end of the Korean War. He also presided over the admission of the forty-ninth and fiftieth states—Alaska and Hawaii.

It was not until they left the White House in 1961 that Dwight and Mamie Eisenhower settled into their first permanent home, a farm in Gettysburg, Pennsylvania. The

These pylon plaques on the Eisenhower Center grounds describe the contributions of the Eisenhower family

seventy-year-old former president wrote his memoirs in between rounds of golf. Despite the relaxed schedule, the general's health began to suffer. He'd survived one heart attack as president and had several more after he retired.

On May 14, 1968, Eisenhower traveled to Washington. Weakened by each successive heart attack, he was admitted to Walter Reed Army Hospital, where he lived out the last ten months of his life. His wife stayed in a suite down the hall. Finally, on March 28, 1969, the old warrior's heart gave out.

Three years earlier, Eisenhower had approved a funeral plan carefully crafted by the Military District of Washington, which has oversight of modern presidential funerals. Each moment of the ceremony was outlined with military precision in a fifty-four-page document, including the timing of the gun salutes and the pace at which the procession would travel down Constitution Avenue. Many of those elements, including the riderless horse preceding the caisson, had been seen just a few years before at the funeral of John Kennedy.

Eisenhower's body was taken to lie in state in the Capitol rotunda. Citizens waited to pay their respects in a line that stretched six city blocks.

In twenty-four hours, fifty-five thousand people passed by the catafalque. President Richard Nixon, who had served as Eisenhower's vice president, gave a eulogy. Government offices closed and flags flew at half mast.

The funeral was held at Washington National Cathedral. Two thousand invited guests filled the church to capacity. Representatives from more than seventy-eight countries attended, including French President Charles De Gaulle. Lyndon Johnson was also there on his first trip to Washington, D.C., since leaving the White House. Thousands more gathered on the lawn in freezing weather to listen to the service over a public address system. Reverend L.R. Elson quoted scripture and the congregation sang "A Mighty Fortress is Our God" and "Onward Christian Soldiers."

After the funeral, Eisenhower's body was taken by train to his hometown, Abilene, Kansas, the site of Eisenhower's presidential library. In Abilene, the hearse passed slowly by Eisenhower's modest boyhood cottage on its way to the library. Thousands lined the route. Three hundred invited guests gathered at the library steps. A minister read Psalms 23 and 121 before the military guard fired its twenty-one-gun salute and the bugler sounded taps. The former president's widow was given the flag that covered his casket.

The walls of the crypt are inscribed with quotes from several of Dwight Eisenhower's speeches

Eisenhower was buried as he wished in his army uniform and in an eighty-dollar standard-issue military coffin. He was laid to rest in the Place of Meditation, one of five buildings in the Eisenhower complex. Later that afternoon, a grieving Mamie Eisenhower returned to the gravesite. She placed a gladiola on her husband's grave and chrysanthemums on her son's. When she died ten years later, she was buried alongside them.

Touring the Tomb at the Dwight D. Eisenhower Library and Museum

The Dwight D. Eisenhower Library and Museum is located in Abilene, Kansas, approximately 150 miles west of Kansas City and 90 miles north of Wichita.

The complex is open daily from 7:45 a.m. until 6:00 p.m. from Memorial Day until mid-August. The rest of the year the opening hours are 9:00 a.m. until 4:45 p.m. The chapel is open year-round from dawn until dusk. All buildings are closed Thanksgiving, Christmas, and New Year's Day. A fee is charged for the museum only. Admission is $8.00 for adults aged sixteen to sixty-one. The fee for senior citizens is $6.00. Children ages eight to fifteen are admitted for $1.00. Children under eight are admitted free.

To reach the Library and Museum: Take Interstate 70 to exit 275. The Library and Museum are located about two miles south of I-70 on KS-15.

For additional information

The Dwight D. Eisenhower Library and Museum
200 SE 4th Street
Abilene, KS 67410
Phone: (785) 263-6700
Fax: (785) 263-6715
www.eisenhower.archives.gov

Eisenhower was eight years old when his family moved into this Abilene, Kansas home

"On the morning of March 28, 1969, the old soldier issued his final command."

—Richard Norton Smith

In 1967 amidst stringent secrecy, the former president traveled to Denver to exhume the remains of his first son, Doud Dwight, known to his doting parents as Icky, who had died of scarlet fever in 1921 at the age of four. The former president, his grief still fresh after four decades, accompanied the small casket to Abilene, Kansas. There he personally supervised Icky's interment near the crypts reserved for himself and Mamie in a plain sandstone chapel across the street from his boyhood home and presidential library.

Thereafter Eisenhower's health deteriorated rapidly. By the spring of 1968, a series of heart attacks led to his hospitalization at Walter Reed. Mamie took up residence in a tiny room next to his suite. One early visitor was the Reverend Billy Graham, whose help Ike sought in patching up an occasionally strained relationship with Richard Nixon. The upshot was Eisenhower's public endorsement of his former vice president before Republican delegates met in Miami Beach that August to choose their presidential candidate. Pleased as he was by Nixon's victory at the polls that fall, he was made even happier by the December nuptials of his grandson David to Nixon's daughter Julie.

As Eisenhower's condition worsened, Billy Graham returned to Walter Reed for a visit. After half an hour of conversation, Ike asked his doctor and nurses to leave the room. Taking the evangelist's hand, he said, "Billy, you've told me how to be sure my sins are forgiven and that I'm going to Heaven. Would you tell me again?"

Graham reached for his copy of the New Testament. He read the old, familiar verses promising eternal life, before adding a short prayer of his own.

"Thank you," said Eisenhower. "I'm ready." On the morning of March 28, 1969, the old soldier issued his final command. After ordering his son and grandson to prop him up in his hospital bed, Ike told John Eisenhower, "I want to go. God take me."

— RNS

Dwight D. Eisenhower

Thirty-fifth President – 1961-1963

Born: May 29, 1917, in Brookline, Massachusetts

Died: 2:00 p.m. on November 22, 1963, in Dallas, Texas

Age at death: 46

Cause of death: Shot by assassin

Final words: Reputed to have said, "My God, I've been hit."

Admission to Arlington National Cemetery: Free

John F. Kennedy was the first president born in the twentieth century. He was also the first Roman Catholic to hold that office. He defeated Vice President Richard Nixon to become the thirty-fifth president of the United States.

Kennedy held that office for just over a thousand days. His administration increased the military advisors in Southeast Asia and faced off with Communist regimes in Cuba, East Germany, and the Soviet Union. At home, Kennedy began work on a legislative program addressing civil rights.

On November 21, 1963, Kennedy and Vice President Lyndon Johnson traveled to Texas on a political salvage mission. After stops in San Antonio and Houston, the party flew to Dallas, where the president was to speak at the Trade Mart. His

An eternal flame burns above the simple plaque bearing John F. Kennedy's dates of birth and death

motorcade made its way from Love Field through downtown Dallas. As it passed the Texas School Book Depository, shots rang out.

The president was struck twice: once in the neck and once in the back of the head. Texas Governor John Connally, riding in front of Kennedy, was also wounded. The car carrying the two wounded men was quickly diverted to Parkland Memorial Hospital.

Efforts to save the president were futile. John F. Kennedy, age forty-six, was pronounced dead at 2:00 p.m. Jacqueline Kennedy, her pink suit stained with her husband's blood, placed her wedding band on his finger. In the waiting area, attention shifted to the new president, Lyndon Johnson.

A few hours later, Johnson was sworn in by Judge Sarah Hughes aboard Air Force One with John Kennedy's coffin in the back of the plane. That afternoon, not far from the Book Depository, Dallas Police Officer J.D. Tippit was shot and killed when he approached a suspect near the assassination scene. The suspect, Lee Harvey Oswald, was captured thirty minutes later.

In Washington, the White House staff acted swiftly. They consulted history books hoping to recreate the majesty of Abraham Lincoln's 1865

John F. Kennedy

state funeral. Kennedy's young widow directed much of the operation. The East Room was bordered in black crepe and decorated with leaves taken from Andrew Jackson's magnolia trees on the South Lawn.

On Sunday, November 24, as Oswald was being transferred from the Dallas city prison to the county jail, Jack Ruby, a local nightclub owner, shot the alleged assassin in the abdomen. NBC beamed live images of the shooting to millions of Americans. Oswald died ninety minutes later. The slain president's family, accompanying JFK's coffin from the White House to the Capitol, was unaware of the latest turn of events.

Waiting in a line that stretched for more than three miles, 250,000 people passed by Kennedy's flag-draped coffin lying in state in the Capitol rotunda. A military guard stood watch over the catafalque, a red, white, and blue wreath from President Johnson resting at its base. Monday morning, nine men from the five armed services carried the casket down the Capitol steps. A military band played "Hail to the Chief," the navy hymn, and Chopin's funeral march as the caisson made its way to the Executive Mansion, where the family, along with hundreds of dignitaries, began a procession to the funeral.

More than a thousand invited guests were packed into St. Matthew's Cathedral. Richard Cardinal Cushing, who had officiated at Kennedy's wedding, performed the requiem mass. Bishop Philip Hannan read scriptural passages and portions of Kennedy's inaugural address.

After the service, the caisson began its journey to Arlington National Cemetery, to a site selected by Mrs. Kennedy overlooking the city. "Black Jack," a riderless horse with boots reversed in its stirrups in honor of a fallen leader, followed behind. John F. Kennedy, Jr., celebrating his third birthday that morning, saluted his father's passing casket. At a graveside service, fifty jets, followed by Air Force One, flew overhead. The widow joined brothers-in-law Robert and Edward Kennedy in lighting the grave's eternal flame.

Jacqueline Kennedy became the first president's widow to receive a staff and Secret Service protection. She was buried alongside her husband when she died in 1994.

On September 24, 1964, the President's Commission on the Assassination of President Kennedy submitted its final report. The investigative panel, known as the Warren Commission after its chairman, Supreme Court Chief Justice Earl Warren, concluded that accused assassin Lee Harvey Oswald acted alone. Many still believe that a larger conspiracy was at work but no conclusive evidence has been found.

Touring John F. Kennedy's Tomb at Arlington National Cemetery

Arlington National Cemetery is open daily, 365 days a year. Hours are from 8:00 a.m. to 7:00 p.m. from April through September and 8:00 a.m. to 5:00 p.m. from October through March. Admission to the cemetery is free.

Arlington National Cemetery is located across the Potomac River from Washington, D.C., at the north end of the Memorial Bridge. The bridge is accessible from Constitution Avenue or Twenty-third Street N.W. near the Lincoln Memorial. The cemetery can also be reached by Metrorail at the Arlington Cemetery stop on the blue line.

Cars are not allowed on the cemetery grounds except by special permission. Paid parking is available near the Visitors Center. Tourmobile offers motorized tours of the cemetery for a fee; Kennedy's gravesite is one of the tour's scheduled stops.

Maps of the cemetery are available at the Visitors Center. To reach Kennedy's grave from the cemetery's main entrance (Memorial Drive), take Roosevelt Drive to Weeks Drive. Signs clearly mark Kennedy's grave.

For additional information

Superintendent
Arlington National Cemetery
Arlington, VA 22211
Visitor Center Phone: (703) 607-8000
www.arlingtoncemetery.org

"For anyone who lived through those four shattering days in November 1963, memory conjures a flawless pageant of grief…" —Richard Norton Smith

Over the years Americans have witnessed with heartbreaking frequency Kennedy funerals. For anyone who lived through those four shattering days in November 1963, memory conjures a flawless pageant of grief, brilliantly choreographed by a young widow. The horse-drawn caisson and riderless horse, the eternal flame, even JFK's interment in Arlington National Cemetery: all were her doing. But the past, as always, informs the present, and with her love of history, it was hardly surprising that Jacqueline Kennedy should turn to the White House Historical Association and its guidebook—both largely her work— with its engraving of the funeral of that nineteenth-century martyr, Abraham Lincoln.

Incredibly, Mrs. Kennedy found time to send condolences to the widow of the Dallas policeman, J.D. Tippit, who was Lee Harvey Oswald's other victim. She held out for St. Matthew's Cathedral and not the massive Shrine of the Immaculate Conception as the site of her husband's funeral. Determined to walk the eight blocks from the White House to St. Matthew's, nothing and no one could change her mind. At first, it was widely assumed that JFK would be laid to rest in his native Massachusetts, in the Brookline cemetery where, a few months

Robert F. Kennedy's cross lies on the slope near his brother's grave in Arlington National Cemetery. In September 2009, Edward M. Kennedy was interred nearby.

Political activist Allard Lowenstein is buried near JFK's grave

earlier, he had buried his infant son Patrick. The Navy was even holding a destroyer in readiness to transport the presidential casket.

Not until Saturday, the twenty-third, a day of incessant downpours and numbing grief, was Kennedy's final resting place decided. While the so-called Irish Mafia pushed for Brookline, Secretary of Defense Robert McNamara thought the Boston area "too parochial." Visiting Arlington National Cemetery, McNamara was captivated by the slope in front of the Lee-Custis Mansion whose stately pillars crowned Arlington's summit. Robert Kennedy was soon converted, as was Jean Kennedy Smith. Returning to the White House that afternoon, she blurted out, "Oh Jackie, we found the most wonderful place!"

Mrs. Kennedy immediately left for Arlington where she, too, fell under its spell. Before evening, work had begun on the gravesite, located on a direct axis with the Lincoln Memorial. By then McNamara had encountered a young college student who worked at the Lee Mansion and who recalled an earlier visit to the site by President Kennedy during which JFK had called the view from the hilltop the most beautiful sight in Washington. It was the ultimate confirmation of McNamara's hunch.

— RNS

Lyndon Baines Johnson

Buried: LBJ Ranch, near Johnson City, Texas

Thirty-sixth President — 1963-1969

Born: August 27, 1908, near Stonewall, Texas

Died: 4:33 p.m. on January 22, 1973, near Johnson City, Texas

Age at death: 64

Cause of death: Heart attack

Final words: Unknown

Admission to LBJ Ranch: Free

On November 22, 1963, Lyndon Baines Johnson became the thirty-sixth president of the United States. Vice President Johnson was riding two cars behind President John F. Kennedy in a Dallas motorcade when an assassin fired shots at JFK. Kennedy was pronounced dead at Parkland Memorial Hospital. A few hours later, as the plane carried the dead president's body back to Washington, Johnson was sworn in by Judge Sarah Hughes aboard Air Force One. First Lady Jacqueline Kennedy and Johnson's wife, Lady Bird, stood at his side. A stunned nation spent the weekend glued to television sets as news of John Kennedy's assassination reached across the globe.

When he arrived in the capital, Lyndon Johnson made his first official statement as president: "This is a sad time for all people. We have suffered a loss that cannot be weighed. For me, it is a deep personal tragedy. I know the world shares the sorrow that Mrs. Kennedy and her family bear. I will do my best. That is all I can do. I ask for your help—and God's."

Johnson's goal was a seamless transition. In a joint session of Congress five days after the assassination, he made an appeal for unity, invoking the memory of the slain president. The following year, he won reelection in his own right. Johnson went on to introduce a broad social program known as the Great Society which addressed poverty, Medicare and Medicaid, and civil rights. Overseas, Johnson agreed to escalate U.S. involvement in Vietnam.

Statue of LBJ on the grounds of his ranch

On March 31, 1968, public outcry over U.S. involvement in Vietnam led Lyndon Johnson to announce his decision not to run for reelection. Instead, he pledged to seek an end to the war in Asia. He would not live to see that goal accomplished. Visibly worn, LBJ returned to his beloved ranch in the Texas Hill Country, making occasional public appearances. In December 1972, Johnson traveled to Independence, Missouri for Harry Truman's funeral.

On January 22, 1973, LBJ was in his bedroom for his regular afternoon nap when he was stricken with a heart attack. He called the switchboard and asked for the head of his Secret Service detail. Two agents arrived with a portable oxygen unit and found Johnson on the floor beside the bed. One of the agents performed mouth-to-mouth resuscitation and an external heart massage in an effort to save the former president.

Lyndon Baines Johnson

Johnson was quickly flown in a family plane to San Antonio International Airport where he was to be taken by ambulance to Brooke Army Medical Center. But it was too late. Lyndon Johnson was pronounced dead at 4:33 p.m. Lady Bird Johnson arrived moments later by helicopter. She was driving home from the Johnson Library when she learned of her husband's heart attack.

Plans for his funeral had been set five years earlier. Funeral services began in Texas with Johnson's body lying in state at the library. Tens of thousands filed past, including many who had known Johnson since childhood. His gray coffin was then flown to Washington to lie in state at the Capitol Rotunda. Forty thousand people passed by the catafalque where President Nixon laid a wreath of carnations.

To the strains of Chopin's funeral march, a military procession led mourners to National City Christian Church, where Johnson often worshipped as president. The service was broadcast over a public address system for those gathered outside. Leontyne Price, the Metropolitan Opera soprano who had performed at Johnson's inauguration, sang two solos.

Lyndon Johnson made a final journey home to his Texas ranch. A cold rain fell on the morning he was laid to rest alongside his parents. Reverend Billy Graham conducted the service under the oak trees on the northern bank of the Pedernales River. An army band played and Anita Bryant sang the "Battle Hymn of the Republic." The Texas National Guard fired a twenty-one-gun salute. Dignitaries and local citizens alike watched as Lady Bird Johnson was given the flag that covered her husband's coffin. Later that afternoon Hubert Humphrey, who had served as Johnson's vice president, and actor Gregory Peck joined the family and other invited guests for coffee and sandwiches at the ranch house.

Lady Bird Johnson remained active in public life after her husband's death, working with several organizations devoted to preserving the Texas landscape. She died in 2007 at the age of ninety-four and was buried at her husband's side on their Texas ranch.

Touring Lyndon Johnson's Tomb at the LBJ Ranch

The LBJ Ranch is located near Johnson City, Texas. The park headquarters and visitor center which give information about Lyndon Johnson's life and presidency, are located in Johnson City. Both facilities are open daily except Thanksgiving, Christmas, and New Year's Day. The visitor center is open from 8:45 a.m. to 5:00 p.m. Bus tours of the LBJ Ranch are available from 10:00 a.m. to 4:00 p.m. Admission to the LBJ Ranch is free. Go to the state park visitor center to receive a free permit to drive through the park. Admission to the Texas White House Office tour is $1.00 for adults and free for children seventeen and younger.

From Austin: Take Highway 290 West. At the traffic light in Johnson City, turn left (still on Highway 290) towards Fredericksburg. Drive three blocks and turn left on Avenue F, then go two blocks and turn right onto Lady Bird Lane. The parking lot and Visitor Center are located on the left.

From San Antonio: Take Highway 281 North until it joins Highway 290. At the traffic light in Johnson City, turn left towards Fredericksburg, drive three blocks and turn left on Avenue F. Go two blocks and turn right onto Lady Bird Lane. The parking lot and Visitor Center are located on the left.

From Fredericksburg: Take Highway 290 East to Johnson City. After passing the blinking traffic light, drive two blocks and turn right onto Avenue F. Go two blocks and turn right onto Lady Bird Lane. The parking lot and Visitor Center are located on the left.

To the LBJ Ranch: From park headquarters, take Highway 290 West fourteen miles to the LBJ State Historical Park. Tickets for the LBJ Ranch bus tour are purchased at the State Park Visitor Center.

Lyndon Johnson's gravesite is beside the ranch house in the Johnson family cemetery along the banks of the Pedernales River.

For additional information

Lyndon B. Johnson National Historical Park
P.O. Box 329
Johnson City, Texas 78636
Phone: (830) 868-7128
Fax: (830) 868-7863
www.nps.gov/lyjo/

Lyndon Baines Johnson

"If ever there were a Lion in Winter, it was Lyndon Johnson." —*Richard Norton Smith*

The Johnson family cemetery on the grounds of the LBJ ranch

If ever there were a Lion in Winter, it was Lyndon Johnson. His post-presidential kingdom shrank to the dimensions of the LBJ Ranch, his white hair grew to near-shoulder length, and memoir writing held little appeal. As he once informed Harry Middleton, the director of his presidential library, in a different context, "Good men have been trying to save my reputation for forty years, and not a damn one succeeded. What makes you think you can?" Haunted by Vietnam, Johnson feared that Richard Nixon's conservative counterrevolution would scuttle his Great Society. "And when she dies," he observed, "I, too, will die."

Death was much on his thoughts. He took the Reverend Billy Graham out to the Johnson family cemetery on the banks of the

Pedernales. "One day you're going to be asked to preach at my funeral," he told Graham. "You'll come right here under this tree and I'll be buried right there. You'll read the Bible and preach the Gospel and I want you to. I hope you'll tell people about some of the things I tried to do."

One of the things Lyndon Johnson tried hardest to do was redress centuries of racial injustice. In December 1971, an obviously ailing former president attended a civil rights conference at the LBJ Library. In the audience were such giants of the movement as Thurgood Marshall, Roy Wilkins, Hubert Humphrey, and Earl Warren. His doctors urged him to stay away; if he had to go, by all means he should avoid the strain of public speaking. Being Lyndon Johnson, he overruled their objections. He had a valedictory message to deliver and it didn't lack for point.

"Progress has been much too small; we haven't done nearly enough," Johnson told his countrymen. "To be black in white society is not to stand on level and equal ground. While the races may stand side by side, whites stand on history's mountain and blacks stand in history's hollow. Until we overcome unequal history, we cannot overcome unequal opportunity."

It was his last public appearance. Among those filing by Johnson's casket at the library six weeks later was a young, bearded man who on another day might have marched in protest of the Vietnam War. Bowing slightly before Lady Bird Johnson, he said simply, "My apologies." Meanwhile, Harry Middleton assigned someone on the library staff to keep a careful count of the thirty-two thousand mourners who came to pay their respects. "I know that somewhere, sometime, President Johnson is going to ask me," he explained.

— RNS

Richard Nixon

Buried: Richard Nixon Library and Birthplace, Yorba Linda, California

Thirty-seventh President – 1969-1974

Born: January 9, 1913, in Yorba Linda, California

Died: 9:08 p.m. on April 22, 1994, in New York, New York

Age at death: 81

Cause of death: Stroke

Final words: Unknown

Admission to Richard Nixon Library and
Birthplace: $9.95

Richard Nixon is the only U.S. president to resign his office. He won the presidency in 1968 on his second try, after narrowly losing the opportunity to succeed Dwight Eisenhower to John F. Kennedy in 1960.

The first Nixon administration focused much of its attention on world affairs, particularly the reduction of U.S. involvement in Vietnam. Nixon visited China, the first U.S. president to do so, in an attempt to restore diplomatic relations with the Communist regime.

However, Nixon's presidency is remembered for the aftermath of events in 1972 connected to his reelection campaign. Several members of his campaign staff were arrested for breaking into the Democratic National Committee at the Watergate complex in Washington. When

Nixon's monument reads, "The greatest title history can bestow is the title of peacemaker"

it was revealed that aides to the president had engaged in a series of illegal schemes, including burglary and wiretapping, a Senate committee was established to investigate. Several of the officials were later convicted for their roles in the Watergate affair.

Tapes from the president's own White House recording system confirmed that he was aware of the crimes and tried to hinder the investigation. In July 1974, the House Judiciary Committee issued three articles of impeachment against the president. He was charged with obstruction of justice, abuse of power, and failure to comply with congressional subpoenas. Rather than risk impeachment, Nixon resigned the presidency on August 9, 1974.

Richard and Pat Nixon returned to their home in San Clemente, California, hoping to escape the glare of publicity. In September 1974, a month after his resignation, Nixon was granted a full pardon by his successor, Gerald Ford. In 1980, the Nixons moved back to the east coast to be closer to their daughters and grandchildren. The former president wrote several bestselling books on foreign policy. As an elder statesman, he continued to travel abroad and to advise successive administrations on foreign policy.

On the afternoon of Monday, April 18, 1994, Richard Nixon, then eighty-one, was relaxing at his Park Ridge, New Jersey home. He'd spent the day crafting a speech to rally the Republican faithful. Around 5:45 p.m., Nixon suffered a massive stroke. His housekeeper, Heidi Retter, helped him to a sofa before calling an ambulance.

Doctors found his right side was paralyzed and his speech and vision impaired. The next morning, he took a turn for the worse.

Richard Nixon

By Thursday, Richard Nixon had fallen into a deep coma. His "living will" forbade the use of any extraordinary measures to prolong his life. With his two daughters and their families at his bedside, Richard Nixon died at 9:08 p.m. on Friday, April 22, 1994. Arrangements were made for a funeral service at the Nixon Library in Yorba Linda, California. At the dedication of the complex just four years earlier, Nixon had spoken to friends of his plan to be "planted" there under an oak tree. Respecting Nixon's wishes, his family declined to mark his death with an elaborate state affair in Washington.

Nixon's plain wooden casket was flown to California on the same Boeing 707 that had carried him into political exile in 1974. Amidst violent thunderstorms, the former president's body was taken by a military honor guard to lie in repose at the library. A military band played "Hail to the Chief," nearly drowned out by the news helicopters circling overhead. Over the next twenty hours, an estimated forty-two thousand people, largely working class, filed past the closed casket, which was surrounded by hundreds of floral tributes, including those sent by Russian President Boris Yeltsin and Poland's Lech Walesa.

On Wednesday, April 27, three thousand guests gathered on the library grounds for the funeral. The four remaining former presidents—Ford, Carter, Reagan, and George H.W. Bush—and their wives joined President and Mrs. Clinton in the first row. More than one hundred members of the U.S. House and Senate attended, along with many foreign dignitaries. Reverend Billy Graham conducted the service, telling of Nixon's final thumbs up to doctors as he entered the hospital. President Clinton read a eulogy, as did California Governor Pete Wilson, Nixon's Secretary of State Henry Kissinger, and Senate Minority Leader Robert Dole, who broke down as he gave his final tribute.

After the "Battle Hymn of the Republic" was played and taps was sounded, the two flags covering the coffin were given to Nixon's daughters. Planes flew overhead and a fifty-gun salute was fired. Richard Nixon was laid to rest alongside his wife Pat, who had died of lung cancer the previous year. His black granite tombstone is inscribed with a quote from his first inaugural address: "The greatest honor history can bestow is the title of peacemaker."

A vast lawn stretches between Herbert Hoover's birthplace and gravesite. Though Hoover lived his final years in New York City, he requested that his final resting place be at his library, within sight of the cottage where he was born in West Branch.

Franklin Delano Roosevelt is buried alongside his wife Eleanor on the grounds of his estate in Hyde Park, New York, two hours north of New York City.

HARRY S. TRUMAN

BORN MAY 8, 1884
LAMAR, MISSOURI
DIED DECEMBER 26, 1972

MARRIED JUNE 28, 1919
DAUGHTER
BORN FEBRUARY 17, 1924

JUDGE
EASTERN DISTRICT
JACKSON COUNTY
JAN. 1, 1923 — JAN. 1, 1925

PRESIDING JUDGE
JACKSON COUNTY
JAN. 1, 1927 — JAN. 1, 1935

UNITED STATES SENATOR
MISSOURI
JAN. 3, 1935 — JAN. 18, 1945

VICE PRESIDENT
UNITED STATES
JAN. 20, 1945 — APR. 12, 1945

PRESIDENT
UNITED STATES
APR. 12, 1945 — JAN. 20, 1953

Harry S. Truman's grave is located at his library in Independence, Missouri, thirty minutes from Kansas City. His gravestone lists his marriage and the birth of his daughter among his accomplishments.

The Place of Meditation on the grounds of the Eisenhower library in Abilene, Kansas, ninety miles north of Wichita, houses the graves of Dwight and Mamie Eisenhower.

"Humility must always be the portion of any man who receives acclaim earned in blood of his followers and sacrifices of his friends."

Guildhall Address, London
June 12, 1945

"Every gun made, every warship launched, every rocket fired signifies, in the final sense, a theft from those who hunger and are not fed, those who are cold and are not clothed . . . . Under This is not a way of life at all . . . . Under the cloud of threatening war, it is humanity hanging from a cross of iron."

"The Chance for Peace" Address, Washington, D.C.
April 16, 1953

(Photo courtesy Eisenhower Library)

Wreath-laying ceremony at the Eisenhower grave on October 16, 1999. The military places flowers at presidential gravesites on each president's birthday. These ceremonies are conducted annually on behalf of the current president.

ABOVE: John F. Kennedy is buried at the foot of a hill beneath Robert E. Lee's mansion on the grounds of Arlington National Cemetery. Kennedy's widow, Jacqueline, modeled the eternal flame at his grave after the one at the Arc de Triomphe in Paris, France.

OPPOSITE: Lyndon Baines Johnson and Lady Bird Johnson are buried in the family cemetery at their Texas ranch, along the banks of the Pedernales River. The LBJ Ranch, deep in the Texas Hill Country, is located ninety minutes west of Austin.

RICHARD NIXON
1913 — 1994
THE GREATEST HONOR HISTORY CAN BESTOW
IS THE TITLE OF PEACEMAKER

The Nixon Library in Yorba Linda, California, an hour from Los Angeles, is the site of the 37th president's birthplace and gravesite.

Touring the Tomb at the Richard Nixon Library and Birthplace

The Richard Nixon Library and Birthplace is open daily, except Thanksgiving, Christmas, and New Years Day. Hours are from 10:00 a.m. to 5:00 p.m., Monday through Saturday, and 11:00 a.m. to 5:00 p.m. on Sundays. Admission is $9.95 for adults, $5.95 for students, $6.95 for senior citizens, and $3.75 for children ages seven to eleven.

From downtown Los Angeles: Go south on Interstate 5 to Highway 91. Take Highway 91 East to Highway 57. Take Highway 57 North and exit at Yorba Linda Boulevard. Turn right on Yorba Linda to reach the library and birthplace.

From LAX: Take Sepulveda to 105 Freeway East. From 105, take 605 Freeway South to 91 Freeway East to 57 Freeway North. Exit at Yorba Linda Boulevard. Turn right on Yorba Linda Boulevard to reach the library and birthplace.

To reach the gravesite, exit the lobby and walk alongside the reflecting pool. The memorial is located at the end of the reflecting pool, directly across from Nixon's birthplace.

For additional information

Richard Nixon Library and Birthplace
18001 Yorba Linda Boulevard
Yorba Linda, CA 92886
Phone: (714) 993-5075
Fax: (714) 528-0544
www.nixonlibraryfoundation.org

Patricia Nixon's inscription reads, "Even when people can't speak your language, they can tell if you have love in your heart"

"The theme was one of reconciliation..."

—*Richard Norton Smith*

In June 1993, I was privileged to join the congregation of mourners who attended Pat Nixon's funeral, held in the rose garden of the Nixon Library in Yorba Linda, California. Afterwards, we were invited inside the library for an impromptu tribute from a grieving husband. Richard Nixon spoke that day of the joys of grandparenting. He remembered how his first grandchild, young Melanie Eisenhower, had been uncertain what to call Pat. Not surprisingly, Mrs. Nixon thought Grandmother overly formal and Grandma a bit too ancient for her liking.

"Why don't you just call me Ma?" Pat told the little girl. Melanie next approached her grandfather with the same question.

"Oh, that's all right, Melanie," the former president replied. "You can call me anything, because I've been called everything."

"Checkers," Nixon's famous dog, is immortalized on the grounds of the Richard Nixon Library

Yorba Linda, California

170

Richard Nixon was born in this Yorba Linda, California home

Looking around, I saw Senator Bob Dole biting his lip, struggling to contain his emotions. A few feet away stood former Senator George McGovern, Nixon's 1972 opponent, dabbing at his eyes with a handkerchief. Later on, McGovern was approached by a reporter crass enough to ask what he was doing at the funeral services. McGovern expressed his longstanding admiration for Mrs. Nixon, only to be reminded of the alleged dirty tricks conducted by the Nixon campaign a generation earlier. The implication was clear: how could he in good conscience honor the wife of such an opponent?

"You can't keep campaigning forever," said McGovern.

The exchange came back to me just ten months later when attending the late president's funeral service at the Nixon Library. Again, the theme was one of reconciliation, unforgettably illustrated by the presence of America's five living presidents and their wives, as well as President Clinton's generous invitation to stop judging America's most controversial president on anything less than his entire record.

— RNS

Gerald R. Ford

Buried: Gerald R. Ford Presidential Museum, Grand Rapids, Michigan

Thirty-eighth President — 1974-1977

Born: July 14, 1913, in Omaha, Nebraska

Died: 6:45 p.m. on December 26, 2006, in Rancho Mirage, California

Age at death: 93

Cause of death: heart disease

Final words: Unknown

Admission to Gerald R. Ford Museum: $7.00

Gerald Ford is the only man in American history to have reached the Oval Office without being elected as either president or vice president. He stood for election in 1976; after narrowly losing, Ford attended Jimmy Carter's inauguration, then said good-bye to his staff. Setting out for the warm temperatures of Palm Springs, California, and a game with legendary golfer Arnold Palmer, he told reporters, "The presidency was hard, but I had anticipated it would be. I had seen presidents before. I had seen the tough jobs they had, the difficult decisions they had to make. So I knew it would be tough. But I have always liked long hours."

Even before his presidency ended, Gerald Ford considered his legacy. On December 13, 1976, Ford wrote to the president of the University of Michigan, his beloved

The Ford Museum in Grand Rapids, Michigan opened its doors in 1981

alma mater, and offered to give all his papers to the federal government, with the understanding that they would be housed in a campus library. He became the first president to donate his papers while still in office. On the last day of his presidency, nine vans filled with 8,500 cubic feet of Gerald Ford's papers headed for Ann Arbor, Michigan.

The library opened in April 1981; the Gerald R. Ford Museum, located in Ford's hometown of Grand Rapids, Michigan, opened in September that same year. Today the library provides researchers with over 20 million documents relating to Ford's presidency. The Ford Museum profiles the former president's life and career with exhibits ranging from a 1970s disco-style theater and full-scale replica of the Oval Office, to the tools used in the Watergate break-in and a holographic White House permitting visitors to go "inside" rooms of the presidential residence. President and Mrs. Ford decided that they would be buried on the museum grounds.

Gerald Ford continued to lead an active life after leaving the White House. He completed his memoirs, frequently contributed to the nation's op-ed pages, and remained involved in Republican Party politics. In August 1999, on the twenty-fifth anniversary of his inauguration, President Ford was awarded the Presidential Medal of Freedom in a ceremony at the White House. Presenting the medal to President Ford, President Bill Clinton said, "When he left the White House after 895 days, America was stronger, calmer, and more self-confident. America was, in other words, more like President Ford himself."

This astronaut at the museum's entrance represents Ford's commitment to America's space program

Mr. Ford died at his home in Rancho Mirage, California, on December 26, 2006, at the age of ninety-three, as our longest-living former president. Only Herbert Hoover had a longer post-presidential life. Mr. Ford's official funeral ceremonies took place over five days, beginning with a public viewing in Palm Desert, California. A national day of mourning was declared by President George W. Bush as Gerald Ford's body lay in state in the U.S. Capitol. A memorial service attended by the four living presidents—Jimmy Carter, George H. W. Bush, Bill Clinton, and George W. Bush—at Washington's National Cathedral honored the former president with cannon and pealing bells. President Ford's body was then flown to his presidential museum in Grand Rapids, Michigan, where 10,000 mourners stood in line for an all-night viewing of the presidential casket. A final memorial service was held at nearby Grace Episcopal Church, where he and Betty had been married, followed by internment at the museum.

Touring the Gerald R. Ford Museum or Library

The Gerald R. Ford Museum is located on the west bank of the Grand River in Grand Rapids, Michigan and is open to the public daily. The Ford Museum is open daily from 9:00 a.m. to 5:00 p.m., except Thanksgiving, Christmas, and New Year's Day. Admission to the museum is $7.00 for adults, $6.00 for senior citizens, and free for children under age sixteen.

To reach the museum from Cadillac or Muskegon: Take Interstate 296/U.S. 131 South and exit at Pearl Street. Turn left on Pearl at the light to the museum entrance. Turn left into the parking lot.

From Lansing: Take Interstate 196 West, also known as the Gerald Ford Freeway. Take the Ottawa/Downtown exit and continue to Pearl Street. Turn right on Pearl Street and right into the parking lot.

From Kalamazoo: Take U.S. 131 North and exit at Pearl Street. Turn right onto Pearl to the museum entrance and north into the parking lot.

The Gerald R. Ford Library is situated on University of Michigan's North Campus in Ann Arbor, Michigan. It is open Monday through Friday, 8:45 a.m. to 4:45 p.m., except federal holidays.

To reach the library: Exit U.S. 23 onto Geddes Road heading west. Geddes Road becomes Fuller Road. Follow Fuller until you reach Beal Avenue. Make a right turn onto Beal Avenue. The first driveway on the right is the entrance to the parking lot. The library has free parking but visitors need to obtain a permit from the front office.

For additional information

Gerald R. Ford Museum
303 Pearl Street NW
Grand Rapids, MI 49504-5353
Phone: (616) 254-0400
Fax: (616) 254-0386
www.ford.utexas.edu

Gerald R. Ford Library
1000 Beal Avenue
Ann Arbor, MI 48109
Phone: (734) 205-0555
Fax: (734) 205-0571
www.ford.utexas.edu

This piece of the Berlin Wall was given to Gerald Ford

> " ... Ford had prided himself on seeking common ground. 'It's all right to be a partisan,' he told one youthful White House aide, 'but not a zealot.'" —*Richard Norton Smith*

In the penultimate years of his life, Gerald Ford often decried the loss of civility poisoning American politics. During his years on Capitol Hill and, subsequently, as president grappling with the demons released by Vietnam and Watergate, Ford had prided himself on seeking common ground. "It's all right to be a partisan," he told one youthful White House aide, "but not a zealot." In part this was generational; like his youthful House colleagues Jack Kennedy and Dick Nixon, Ford's pragmatic outlook was shaped by his World War II experiences, and by the subsequent Cold War consensus that subordinated domestic differences to the superpower rivalry. Ironically, when the Berlin Wall came down in 1989, so did many of our self-imposed restraints. The Cold War gave way to Culture Wars, more intensely waged than disputes over economic or foreign policy, if only because the ground being contested involved values rather than numbers.

Against this increasingly polarized backdrop, presidents as dissimilar as Bill Clinton and George W. Bush found their legitimacy disputed in terms bordering on the apocalyptic.

This wasn't Gerald Ford's style. His funeral would serve to remind his countrymen of a time, not so distant, when success in politics was defined as narrowing differences, not exploiting them. First things first. "Keep it simple," Mrs. Ford remarked at an early planning meeting I attended, "and remember the family." The Fords selected favorite verses of scripture to be read, and hymns that had special meaning for them. The marvelous mezzo-soprano Denyce Graves accepted an invitation to perform The Lord's Prayer at Washington's National Cathedral. Penciled in for the Grand Rapids church service was the Army Chorus. Though generally amenable to the program outlined by military planners, Ford was adamantly

Grand Rapids and Ann Arbor, Michigan

opposed to a horse drawn caisson on Constitution Avenue, or anywhere else. Efforts to change his mind met with a predictable stone wall of resistance. Not only did we remember the family; the family had its own defining memories. In lieu of the aforementioned caisson, the hearse carrying the former president's remains would drive through Alexandria neighborhoods in which the Fords had once lived. Later it would pause at the recently completed World War II Memorial, affording veterans an opportunity to salute their colleague and former commander-in-chief.

Again breaking with tradition, at the Capitol the casket would enter the building on the House side, this in recognition of Ford's quarter century pursuit of the one Washington job he really wanted— Speaker of the House. Once the period of public viewing concluded, he would leave by way of the Senate, a symbolic tribute to his unique status as a Man of the House who also presided, however briefly, over The Other Body. Among his Washington eulogists, Ford counter-

intuitively wished to include a journalist. His original choice, Time's Hugh Sidey, died before he could carry out his assignment. A worthy replacement was identified in Tom Brokaw, whose career as a White House correspondent coincided with the Ford presidency. By the time these plans were actually implemented, they seemed almost eerily prescient; rarely had Americans been so divided as at the end of 2006. The ceremonies attending the death of a president long out of office, and not much in the public eye of late, provided an opportunity to come together.

Michigan was to be a homecoming, with Air Force One flying low over the Ann Arbor football stadium where young Junie Ford had attracted notice from pro scouts. Greeting the plane's arrival in Grand Rapids, the Wolverine band offered a solemn rendition of Hail to the Victors, the Michigan fight song that had briefly displaced Hail to the Chief in the autumn of 1974. That night over 60,000 people braved the January cold, in lines stretching two miles from the Ford Museum where the town's favorite son passed his final night. Don Rumsfeld spoke at the concluding church service on

January 3, but so did Jimmy Carter, recalling in moving words his unlikely friendship with the man he defeated in the 1976 election. (Anyone questioning the depth of feeling between this political odd couple should have seen President Carter pacing the aisles of Air Force One while cradling Gerald Ford's infant great-grandchild in his arms.)

In my own concluding remarks, I recalled the 2001 presentation to Ford of the John F. Kennedy Profiles in Courage Award in recognition of his politically-suicidal decision to pardon Richard Nixon. Eight years later, Ted Kennedy's generous words on that occasion came back to me as Americans marked the senator's passing and reflected on yet another historical chapter closed. More than mere bipartisanship, such linkages attest not only to the democracy of death, but to the lifeblood of democracy. They invite reflection on what is transitory and what is timeless. Can you think of a better definition of perspective?

— RNS

Richard Norton Smith at the Ford Museum in Grand Rapids, Michigan

Grand Rapids and Ann Arbor, Michigan

Jimmy Carter

Thirty-ninth President – 1977-1981

Born: October 1, 1924, in Plains, Georgia

Presidential library and museum: The Jimmy Carter Presidential Library and Museum, Atlanta, Georgia

Admission to Jimmy Carter Presidential Library and Museum: $8.00

Jimmy Carter's last day as president was a race against the clock. On January 20, 1981, after months of intense negotiations, Iran signaled that it was prepared to free fifty-two American hostages who had been held for 444 days. But an hour and a half before noon on inauguration day, Iran had still not released the plane with the hostages on board. Time had run out for the Carter administration. At 10:45 a.m., Rosalynn Carter entered the Oval Office to tell her husband that the Reagans were arriving; it was time to pack up and dress for the ceremonies. At 12:33 p.m., as Ronald Reagan concluded his inaugural address, the Secret Service alerted Jimmy Carter that Iran had released the plane. Mr. Carter would later write in his memoirs *Keeping Faith*, "I was overwhelmed with happiness—but because of the hostages' freedom, not mine."

Following his successor's inauguration, Jimmy Carter returned to his hometown of Plains, Georgia. Since then, Jimmy Carter has stayed active in international affairs, written over fifteen books, and is a regular volunteer for Habitat for Humanity, a nonprofit organization that builds homes for low-income families.

The entrance to Carter Presidential Center in Atlanta

On October 2, 1984, Jimmy Carter broke ground outside of downtown Atlanta for his largest project—the Carter Library and Museum and the Carter Center. The museum recently underwent a $10 million overhaul and formally reopened to the public on President Carter's eighty-fifth birthday, October 1, 2009. It now devotes more space than any other presidential library to life after the Oval Office; about a third of the museum is dedicated to Mr. Carter's life after he was defeated by Ronald Reagan in 1980. Since its original opening, the museum has drawn thousands of visitors annually. Researchers at the Carter Center, housed in the same complex, can explore issues such as human rights, conflict resolution, and health policy.

Mr. Carter is not likely to be buried at his library, saying in a 2006 C-SPAN interview that he and Rosalynn would be buried near their home in Plains, Georgia. "Plains is special to us. I could be buried in Arlington Cemetery or wherever I want, but my wife was born here and I was born here."

As for his place in history Jimmy Carter would like to "… be remembered for things that [I] did that contributed to peace and human

This statue on the grounds of the complex commemorates Carter's battle against the guinea worm in Africa

Atlanta, Georgia   **180**

rights. I'd like people to understand that I have been honest and truthful, that I've loved the simpler things of life." In 2002, Mr. Carter was awarded the Nobel Peace Prize for his work promoting human rights and international peace.

The museum houses a replica of Carter's Oval Office

Touring the Jimmy Carter Presidential Library and Museum and The Carter Center

The Carter Library and Museum and the Carter Center are located in one complex in Atlanta, Georgia, two miles from downtown. The Library and Museum is open Monday through Friday from 8:30 a.m. to 4:30 p.m. Admission to the Library and Museum is $8.00 for adults, $6.00 for senior citizens, military, and students with ID, and free for children age sixteen and under.

To reach the complex from the north or south: Take Interstate 75/85 to exit 248C, the Freedom Parkway. Follow the signs to the Carter Complex.

From the east or west: Take I-20 to Moreland Avenue North. Turn left on Freedom Parkway. Follow the signs to the Carter Complex.

For additional information

The Jimmy Carter Presidential Library and Museum
441 Freedom Parkway
Atlanta, Georgia 30307-1498
Phone: (404) 865-7100
www.jimmycarterlibrary.org

The Carter Center
453 Freedom Parkway
Atlanta, GA 30307
(404) 331-3900
www.cartercenter.org

Ronald Reagan

Buried: Ronald Reagan Library, Simi Valley, California

Fortieth President—1981-1989
Born: February 6, 1911, in Tampico, Illinois
Died: 1:00 p.m. on June 5, 2004, in Bel-Air, California
Age at death: 93
Cause of death: pneumonia, complicated
by Alzheimer's disease
Final words: Unknown
Admission to Ronald Reagan Presidential
Library and Museum: $12.00

On January 20, 1989, Ronald Reagan took a final look at the Oval Office and remarked how bare it was. The fortieth president had served two terms in office, survived an assassination attempt, and at the age of seventy-seven was the oldest man to leave the presidency. He watched as his vice president, George Bush, took the oath to succeed him. Then, Ronald Reagan, the most popular president to leave the White House since Dwight D. Eisenhower, retired to his ranch in Bel Air, California.

Ronald Reagan selected one hundred acres of undeveloped land, high in the Simi foothills, north of Los Angeles for the site of his library and museum. On November 4, 1991, former

A piece of the Berlin Wall, the subject of one of Ronald Reagan's most famous speeches

presidents Richard Nixon, Gerald Ford, Jimmy Carter, and President George Bush attended the dedication of the Ronald Reagan Library and Museum. Reagan told his audience, "The doors of this library are open now and all are welcome. The judgment of history is left to you—the people. I have no fears of that, for we have done our best...."

The library and museum contains 50 million documents relating to Reagan's presidency. There is a wall of movie posters from Reagan's Hollywood years featuring *Bedtime for Bonzo, Stallion Road,* and *Hasty Heart,* and photos of young Reagan as a life guard, a radio sports announcer, and a movie star. Visitors also can see a replica of the Oval Office, watch a panoramic video on Reagan's legacy, and read a telegram to Reagan from the parents of his attempted

The Ronald Reagan Library and Museum is located in the hills of Simi Valley, California

assassin John Hinckley. The First Lady's Gallery details Nancy Reagan's life and contributions.

In November 1994, Ronald Reagan wrote a formal farewell letter to the country, revealing that he was afflicted with Alzheimer's disease and would be leaving public life. He wrote, "When the Lord calls me home whenever that may be, I will leave with the greatest love for this country of ours and eternal optimism for its future. I now begin the journey that will lead me into the sunset of my life. I know that for America there will always be a bright dawn ahead."

Ronald Reagan passed away on June 5, 2004, at his home in Bel-Air, California, at the age of ninety-three. His wife, Nancy, and two of his children, Ron and Patti, were by his side. Only one president, Gerald Ford, lived longer. Reagan's passing touched off a week of memorial ceremonies ranging from Southern California to Washington, D.C., and back again. Following a brief, private ceremony for family members at his presidential library in Simi Valley, California, the public was first

The rose garden in front of the Reagan gravesite

Ronald Reagan is buried in this tomb bearing the presidential seal

able to pay their respects as Reagan's casket lay in repose; over 100,000 mourners visited the library over the course of two days.

From California, Nancy Reagan accompanied her husband's casket on a flight to Washington, D.C., for the first state funeral held since Lyndon Johnson's in 1973. In the Capitol rotunda, Reagan's casket was displayed on a catafalque built in 1865 for the funeral of Abraham Lincoln. Mourners waited in line for hours to file past the coffin. President George W. Bush declared Friday, June 11, a day of mourning as Reagan's cortege proceeded from the Capitol along a five-mile route to the National Cathedral. Thousands of onlookers lined the D.C. streets. The service drew notable statesmen and-women from around the world, including all living former presidents and first ladies, British Prime Minister Tony Blair, and Russia's Mikhail Gorbachev. The coffin was flown back to California, where Ronald Reagan was buried at his presidential library during a sunset service for 700 guests.

Ronald Reagan

Touring the Ronald Reagan Presidential Library and Museum

The Ronald Reagan Library and Museum, in Simi Valley, California, is open daily, excluding Thanksgiving, Christmas, and New Year's Day, from 10:00 a.m. to 5:00 p.m. Admission is $12.00 for adults, $9.00 for senior citizens, $3.00 for children ages eleven to seventeen, and free for children ages ten and under.

From Los Angeles and points south: Take I-405 North toward Sacramento to 118 West. Exit at Madera Road South, then turn right on Madera and proceed three miles to Presidential Drive.

From Santa Barbara and points north: Take 101 South to 23 North and exit at Olsen Road. Turn right on Olsen and proceed two miles to Presidential Drive.

Follow Presidential Drive up the hill to the library and look for parking signs.

For additional information

The Ronald Reagan Presidential Library and Museum
40 Presidential Drive
Simi Valley, CA 93065
Phone: (800) 410-8354
www.reagan.utexas.edu

"... ... Reagan himself had often likened politics to show business." —*Richard Norton Smith*

*T*hough ill with Alzheimer's disease for nearly a decade at the time of his death in June 2004, Ronald Reagan had enjoyed a renaissance of popular and scholarly approval. Against the twilight of Reagan's slow fade, many a journalist and academic—some more grudgingly than others—came to reconsider dismissive assessments made at the end of the Reagan presidency. This was not without irony, since Reagan himself had often likened politics to show business. In both occupations, he liked to say, success required a big opening and an equally dramatic close. As good as his word, when he slipped away on June 5, it was not before a stunning moment of emotional connection with the woman who had shared his life for nearly half a century. As Nancy Reagan looked on, her husband opened his eyes before he closed them for the last time. He saw her. His wordless gesture communicated volumes to those by his bedside.

While the circumstances surrounding this president's passing could not have differed more from the horror and convulsive grief of November 1963, there was in both deaths a sense of history transcending mere headlines, of legends in the making. For millions of admirers, Ronald Reagan had become an iconic figure. Sensing the climax of a decisive chapter in the national story, they lined up for hours to ride buses to the mountaintop Reagan Library in Simi Valley, forty miles northwest of Los Angeles. They stood five-and six-deep on the streets of Washington, a town not generally seen as a hotbed of Reaganesque politics. At such times presidential historians find themselves much in demand. As a former director of the Reagan Presidential Library, I returned my share of press calls that week. But I also wanted to get out of the television studio, to experience for myself the street level response generated by Reagan's passing.

So a little after 8 o'clock on a warm June evening I joined the shuffling line outside the Capitol waiting to pay its respects. It snaked down the Hill, past the charging bronze figure of Ulysses S. Grant, beyond the granite lined pools of water which imperfectly connect the sloping Capitol grounds to the adjoining Mall. The moonlit dome, rushed to completion as a symbol of national unity amidst a brutal civil war, provided the perfect backdrop for a National Review *Woodstock*. By the time I walked into the rotunda, shortly before two in the morning, I had conversed with dozens of strangers, many barely old enough to have personal recollections of a presidency that had ended fifteen years before. There were families with strollers and military personnel in uniform; a carload of college kids who had driven from New Jersey; a woman from Missouri, who hadn't slept since leaving home an indeterminate number of hours earlier. Periodically cameramen and microphone-wielding

Nancy Reagan is presented with an American flag at her husband's funeral

journalists invaded our ranks. Reagan stories were told. Old recordings of speeches drifted on the soft spring night. A friend's cell phone allowed us to share the experience with the randomly called.

It was one of those increasingly rare water cooler moments, a mélange of patriotic pride and spirituality and the humbling perspective that comes with confronting our mortality. But if politics were briefly adjourned, democracy was not. Even now, angry, sometimes profane dissents were being registered online and via that defining instrument of electronic populism, the call-in show. Appearing the next day on C-SPAN's Washington Journal I received a couple such jabs myself. Would similar abuse, I wondered, albeit from the opposite end of the political spectrum, have greeted the demise of Jimmy Carter or Bill Clinton? Probably. For in the über partisan climate of recent years—wherein adversaries are routinely treated as enemies, and the clash of ideas can all too easily morph into ideological jihad—death itself cannot instill good manners, let along the unity of grief.

— RNS

George Bush

Forty-first President – 1989-1993
Born: June 12, 1924, in Milton, Massachusetts
Presidential library and museum: The George Bush
Presidential Library and Museum,
College Station, Texas
Admission to George Bush Presidential
Library and Museum: $7.00

On January 20, 1989, George Herbert Walker Bush became the first incumbent vice president to ascend to the presidency since Martin Van Buren in 1836. Mr. Bush continued to follow in Van Buren's footsteps by losing his bid for a second term. On January 20, 1993, George Bush watched Bill Clinton take the oath of office and then retired to his adopted hometown of Houston, Texas. "It's been one hell of a ride," he told a crowd of five hundred people who arrived at the airport to welcome him home.

Since retiring, Mr. Bush has taken a few flying leaps—out of a plane. On March 25, 1997, George Bush began celebrating milestone birthdays by parachuting out of an airplane—this jump over the Arizona desert. After reaching the ground safely, he told reporters, "It was wonderful. I'm a new man. I go home exhilarated." He jumped again, over his presidential library, for his eightieth birthday, and marked his eighty-fifth birthday, on June 12, 2009, with a jump over Maine.

As a World War II navy pilot, he had been forced to bail out of his crippled bomber, badly cutting himself and tearing his chute. The two crewmen with him died.

The George Bush Presidential Library and Museum is located on the grounds of Texas A&M University in College Station, Texas

The parachute Mr. Bush used for his jump during World War II can be seen, along with exhibits chronicling the life and times of the forty-first president, in the George Bush Presidential Library and Museum in College Station, Texas. The library and museum, located on ninety acres of the Texas A&M University campus, was dedicated on November 6, 1997. The library contains more than 40 million of President Bush's papers. The museum features a model of George Bush's Camp David office, displays some of the eighty thousand gifts received by the Bushes, and recreates key events from Bush's White House years.

George and Barbara Bush plan to be buried at the library. Their tomb is already constructed, and located at the back of the library. Made from Texas limestone, it is surrounded by a wrought iron gate decorated with the Star of Texas.

Since leaving the White House, the former president and first lady have traveled to over forty-five countries and done extensive fundraising for charities. "There is no way Barbara and I can be happier in our private lives, none," Mr. Bush has said. "After thirty years in politics, I don't miss it." But he is proud that his sons George W. and Jeb entered the political arena. "If it weren't for [my sons' public service], I might have some kind of itch, not about running again but maybe more involvement."

With the 2000 election, George Bush entered the history books again, joining John Adams as the only presidents to have their sons elected to the presidency. On January 20, 2001, a teary-eyed George Herbert Walker Bush stood watching as his son, George W. Bush, took the oath of office on the west front of the U.S. Capitol.

College Station, Texas

This bridge leads to the site where George and Barbara Bush will be buried

Touring the George Bush Presidential Library and Museum

The George Bush Library and Museum in College Station, Texas is open daily except Thanksgiving, Christmas, and New Year's Day. Hours are Monday through Saturday, 9:30 a.m. to 5:00 p.m., and Sundays from noon to 5:00 p.m. Admission to the museum is $7.00 for adults, $3.00 for students, $6.00 for senior citizens, and free for children under six.

To reach the library from Houston: Take I-45 North to Conroe. In Conroe, take 105 West to Navasota. From Navasota, follow Highway 6 North to Bryan/College Station. Take the Business 6/Texas Avenue exit. At the second light, take a left onto FM 2818. Go approximately four miles, then take a right onto George Bush Drive. The entrance to the Bush Library is on the left.

To reach the library from Dallas: Take I-45 South to Madisonville and take Route 21 West to Bryan/College Station. At the junction of Route 21 and FM 2818, take a left onto FM 2818. Continue on for approximately six miles, then turn left onto George Bush Drive. The entrance to the Bush Library is on the left.

This presidential seal marks the future gravesite

For additional information

The George Bush Presidential Library and Museum
1000 George Bush Drive West
College Station, TX 77845
Phone: (979) 691-4000
Fax: (979) 691-4050
TTY: (979) 691-4091
www.bushlibrary.tamu.edu

George Bush

William Jefferson Clinton

Forty-second President – 1993-2001
Born: August 19, 1946, in Hope, Arkansas
Presidential Library and Museum: Little Rock, Arkansas

On On January 20, 2001, Bill Clinton watched as his successor, George W. Bush, took the oath of office. At age fifty-four, he became one of the youngest men to leave the presidency. The former president and Mrs. Clinton moved to Chappaqua, New York, and Mrs. Clinton entered the history books as the first former first lady to be elected to the U.S. Senate. After her own presidential bid, Hillary Clinton was appointed to another president's cabinet, serving as Barack Obama's secretary of state.

On February 12, 1997, Bill Clinton joined the ranks of other modern presidents in overseeing the creation of his presidential library. Mr. Clinton announced his selection of Little Rock, Arkansas, as the library's future site. Little Rock is not the president's hometown, but the Arkansas capital was his political epicenter in the years before he came to Washington. Bill Clinton served as the state's attorney general for two years and as its governor for almost twelve years before being elected president in 1992.

Boyhood home of Bill Clinton

The Clinton Foundation broke ground for the Presidential Center on December 5, 2001, located on twenty-seven acres of downtown land along the south bank of the Arkansas River, which had been offered by the city of Little Rock. The center opened on November 18, 2004, with a ceremony that included speeches from former presidents George Bush and Jimmy Carter and the sitting president, George W. Bush. Bono of the rock band U2 performed and Nelson Mandela sent a video message as part of the rain-soaked ceremony.

Like most presidential libraries, President Clinton's is operated by the National Archives and Records Administration. Its archives are the largest in American presidential history, holding over 78 million pages of personal papers and official documents and two million photographs. The complex also includes a museum with a full-scale replica of the Oval Office, a timeline of the Clinton presidency, and other exhibits about life in the Clinton White House. The complex is also home to the University of Arkansas Clinton School of Public Service and will serve as a research and education facility on policy initiatives.

Although not an announced part of the Clinton library's planning, it is likely that the site will serve, as have other presidential libraries, as Bill Clinton's final resting place.

Bill Clinton was the only Democrat since Franklin Roosevelt to be elected to a second term in his own right. On December 19, 1998, he also made history

The Clinton presidential library is located in his home state of Arkansas

William Jefferson Clinton

as the second president to be impeached by the U.S. House of Representatives, which passed one count of perjury and another of obstruction of justice. The Senate later voted, largely along party lines, to acquit. Asked about his legacy during a 1997 interview for NBC's *Meet the Press*, President Clinton remarked, "I think a president's legacy is ultimately determined after he's gone from office, and maybe after he's gone from this earth, when people can read all the records and see the real significance of what happened with the benefit of hindsight and without any prejudice for or against [that individual]."

After leaving office in 2001, Bill Clinton has pursued an active post-presidency. He opened an office in Harlem and travels extensively for charity causes and public speaking engagements. In 2004, he published a best-selling autobiography, *My Life*. That year, he was diagnosed with heart disease, resulting in quadruple bypass surgery. In 2005, he formed the Clinton Global Initiative, an organization that aims to bring together government and business leaders, charities, and non-profit organizations to address issues such as poverty, health, education, and climate change.

Touring the William J. Clinton Presidential Center

The William J. Clinton Presidential Center is open daily except Thanksgiving, Christmas, and New Year's Day. Hours are Monday through Saturday, 9:00 a.m. to 5:00 p.m., and Sunday 1:00 p.m. to 5:00 p.m. Admission to the Clinton Center is $7.00 for adults, $5.00 for senior citizens, $5.00 for college students (with valid ID), $3.00 for youth ages six to seventeen, and free for children under six. Admission price for retired military personnel is $5.00 and active military is free. The Center offers four free admission days each year: President's Day, the Fourth of July, the Saturday prior to President Clinton's birthday (August 19), and the Saturday prior to the Center's Grand Opening anniversary (November 18). Audio tours narrated by President Clinton can be purchased for an additional $3.00.

To reach the Clinton Center from north of Little Rock: From I-40, use the I-30 exit and get off Exit 141A Cantrell/Clinton Avenue (the first exit after crossing the Arkansas River). Follow the sign to 2nd Street/Ferry Road. Turn left on Ferry Road and then right on President Clinton Avenue.

To reach the Clinton Center from south of Little Rock: From I-30, take exit 140 (Ninth Street/Sixth Street) and continue on the service road until you reach Third Street. Turn right on Third Street, take the second left onto Dean Kumpuris Street, then turn right on President Clinton Avenue.

For additional information

William J. Clinton Presidential Center
1200 President Clinton Ave.
Little Rock, AR 72201
Phone: (501) 374–4242
www.clintonpresidentialcenter.com

George W. Bush

Forty-third President – 2001–2009

Born: July 6, 1946, in New Haven, Connecticut

On January 20, 2001, George W. Bush took office after a long, contested election. On election night, it became clear that the vote in Florida was too close to call, leaving Florida's crucial 25 electoral votes in question and the race between Mr. Bush and Democratic opponent Al Gore unresolved. After a legal battle between the Bush and Gore camps over hand recounts in Florida, the U.S. Supreme Court ruled the Florida recounts unconstitutional in a 5-4 decision, ending Gore's bid for the presidency about one month after election night.

Among those watching George W. Bush take the oath of office was his father, former president George H. W. Bush. Not since John and John Quincy Adams had a father and son both served as president. Politics runs in the Bush family: Prescott Bush, George W.'s grandfather, was a U.S. senator from Connecticut and his brother Jeb was elected governor of Florida.

After earning an MBA from Harvard in 1975, George W. Bush had an early, unsuccessful flirtation with politics when he ran for Congress in 1978; he then concentrated on the oil business from his base in Midland, Texas. He sold the business and left Midland to help his father, the sitting vice president, win the 1988 presidential election. George W. then returned to Texas and served as managing general partner of the Texas Rangers baseball franchise from 1989 until 1994.

In 1994, he was elected governor of Texas; four years later, he became the first Texas governor to be elected to two consecutive four-year terms, winning 68 percent of the vote.

The historic 2000 presidential election was soon eclipsed by another history-making event when, on September 11, 2001, nineteen Muslim extremists commandeered four U.S. airliners; three were flown into landmark buildings, and the fourth crashed, killing thousands of civilians. Just months after a presidential campaign that had focused on domestic issues, President Bush was to declare a long-term war against international terrorism.

In February of 2008, it was officially announced that Laura Bush's alma mater, Southern Methodist University in Dallas, Texas, would be the home of the George W. Bush Presidential Library and Museum. Groundbreaking is planned for late 2010 with an anticipated completion date in 2013. In November of 2009, Mr. Bush introduced the new George W. Bush Institute, also located at Southern Methodist University, as a forum for study and advocacy in four main areas: education, global health, human freedom, and economic growth. Since retirement, the Bushes have lived nearby in University Park as well as on their ranch in Crawford, Texas. There have been no plans announced publicly for their burial locations.

For additional information

Visit www.georgebushlibrary.com for information about the George W. Bush Presidential Center, including the library, museum, and the George W. Bush Policy Institute.

Barack Obama

Forty-fourth President – 2009-Present
Born: August 4, 1961, in Honolulu, Hawaii

Barack Obama made history as the United States' first African-American president when he was elected on November 4, 2008, defeating Republican Arizona Senator John McCain. The match-up was widely seen as generational, with the forty-six-year-old Obama facing the seventy-one-year-old McCain, who, if elected, would have been the oldest U.S. president. In an atmosphere of economic crisis and war, there was the highest voter turnout in forty years, with Senator Obama winning 68 percent of the electoral votes. Mr. Obama, the one-term, junior Democratic Senator from Illinois, ran under a slogan of "change" and used multimedia campaigning, particularly aimed at younger voters, to an extent that had not been possible in the past.

Barack Obama was born in Hawaii to a Kenyan father, Barack Obama, Sr., and an American mother, Stanley Ann Dunham, though his parents separated when he was two and later divorced. His mother remarried, and in 1967, the family moved to Indonesia with his stepfather. The young Obama, known then as Barry, remained there until at age ten he returned to Hawaii, where he lived with his maternal grandparents. He finished his education through high school at Punahou School, a private college preparatory school. He attended Occidental College in Los Angeles for two years and then transferred to Columbia University in New York, where he was awarded a degree in political science in 1983.

In 1985, he moved to Chicago, where he was a community organizer on the city's south side, working to improve living conditions for the city's poor. He attended Harvard Law School and was named the president of the *Harvard Law Review*. During this time, he met his future wife, Michelle, when he served as a summer associate at the law firm where she worked. They married in 1992 and now have two daughters: Sasha and Malia.

After law school, Mr. Obama returned to Chicago to teach constitutional law at the University of Chicago and work as a civil rights lawyer. It was during this time he ran for the Illinois state senate, where he served for eight years representing Chicago's south side. Barack Obama ran unsuccessfully for a seat in the U.S. House of Representatives in 2000; four years later, he was elected to the U.S. Senate. During that campaign Barack Obama was introduced to the nation when he was selected to deliver the keynote address at the 2004 Democratic National Convention.

Barack Obama authored two bestselling books, *Dreams from My Father* (1995) and *The Audacity of Hope* (2006). In February 2007, he launched his presidential bid in a crowded democratic field that included former first lady, Senator Hillary Rodham Clinton.

As it is still early in President Obama's term, no public plans have been revealed for his presidential library. He does have a variety of locations to choose from, though, that have played a part in his past. With his close connections to Chicago, some are predicting that he will choose the University of Chicago, where he taught.

President Obama's private home in the Kenwood section of Chicago, Illinois. (Jeff Haynes/Polaris)

Barack Obama

Gerald R. Ford's final resting place at the Ford Museum in Grand Rapids, Michigan. (*Courtesy Gerald R. Ford Presidential Museum*)

This train depot in Plains, Georgia, served as the headquarters for Jimmy Carter's 1976 presidential campaign. President Carter plans to be buried at his home in Plains. (*Courtesy Jimmy Carter Presidential Library*)

Ronald Reagan is buried in this tomb on the grounds of the Reagan Library. The library is located in Simi Valley, California, less than one hour from Los Angeles.

George and Barbara Bush will be buried at this site on the grounds of
the Bush Library. The library is on the Texas A&M University campus in
College Station, about ninety minutes north of Houston.

The William J. Clinton Presidential Center opened in 2004 on the south bank of the Arkansas River in Little Rock and is home to a library, museum, and the University of Arkansas Clinton School of Public Service. *(Courtesy William J. Clinton*

ABOVE: President Obama's private home in the Kenwood section of
Chicago, Illinois. (*Jeff Haynes/Polaris*)

OPPOSITE: The George W. Bush Presidential Center will be built on
the campus of Southern Methodist University in Dallas, Texas.
(*Photo © SMU; photo by Hillsman Jackson*)

Local legend has it that Senate President Pro Tempore Atchison was "President for a Day"—March 4, 1849—when incoming President Zachary Taylor refused to be sworn in on a Sunday. Unfortunately for Atchison, U.S. Senate Historian Richard Baker says the story is just that—legend.

Hollywood Cemetery in Richmond, Virginia is the final resting place of Jefferson Davis, president of the Confederate States of America from 1861–1865.

Afterword

by Presidential Historian Douglas Brinkley

We must have many Lincoln-hearted men.
A city is not builded in a day.
And they must do their work, and come and go,
While countless generations pass away.

—Vachel Lindsay,
  "Abraham Lincoln Walks At Midnight"
  (1914)

Whenever I took a group of college students on one of my "Majic Bus" academic treks across America in the 1990s, our primary goal was to study history where it happened and literature where it was created. We always made a pilgrimage to Abraham Lincoln's Tomb in Springfield, Illinois. Much like Lincoln himself, there is something mournful in Springfield's wholesome bond with our greatest president, as if generations of its denizens have remained in a state of perpetual sorrow over his shocking assassination just six days after General Robert E. Lee surrendered the Confederate Army to Union Commander Ulysses S. Grant.

It was as if the people of Springfield had been attending a 138-year wake. The city's downtown was a commercial monument to the martyr of the Civil War, whose likeness is everywhere: on savings and loan signs and fast food billboards, on restaurant menus and flea-market posters, on taxicab doors and bowling-alley walls. A riffle through the Springfield *Yellow Pages* turned up the Lincolnland Baptist Church and Lincoln Rent-a-Car, Lincoln Land Plumbing and Lincoln Pest Control, a Lincoln Chiropractic Clinic, and the Lincoln Dialysis Center. Yet despite this robust commerce, Springfield's Lincoln was not the vigorous young rail-splitter of New Salem or the precocious country lawyer with the brooding eyes, big hands, and a book under each arm, but the dead president lain out in his Sunday best in a velvet-lined open coffin, arms folded across his chest, his face powdered, a small patch of dried blood in his hair—not the man, just the carcass he came in.

With the possible exception of John F. Kennedy's death nearly a century later, Lincoln's death on April 15, 1865, had a greater impact than any other in American history. Shot in his seat at Washington, D.C.'s Ford Theatre while watching the hit play *Our American Cousin,* Lincoln died the day after actor John Wilkes Booth fired a lead ball into his head. The book of Genesis says it took the Israelites forty days to embalm the body of Jacob; Americans needed just one day to do the same for Lincoln's from which the brain and scalp were removed beforehand. The president's corpse was then dressed in a black suit and placed in a lead-lined mahogany casket covered in black broadcloth and studded with silver handles. Lilies, roses, and magnolia blossoms adorned the catafalque around Lincoln's body as it lay in state in the East Room of the White House. Those who viewed the dead president reported that his expression was one of blissful repose.

What has always fascinated me most about the death of Abraham Lincoln is the 1,700-mile journey his coffin made from Washington, D.C. to Springfield, Illinois, a grim train procession detailed in Ralph Newman's 1965 article "In This Sad World of Ours, Sorrow Comes to Us All: A Timetable for the Lincoln Funeral Train," published in the *Journal of the Illinois State Historical Society.* Today it's hard to imagine a slain president's body being taken on a multi-city tour, paraded up Baltimore's Eutaw Street for a public viewing at the Exchange Building, then to another appearance before another mob at Independence Hall in

Philadelphia, and onto the waiting crowds in Harrisburg, Lancaster, Buffalo, Cleveland, Columbus, Indianapolis, and Chicago until the casket finally arrived at the State Capitol in Springfield, where 75,000 people would pass by the bier. Lincoln's body was the hottest ticket in America. Hairs from his head became prized collectibles; his assistant John Hay, for example, had a special ring made with a few dark strands. The level of this obsession with Lincoln's death lives on to this day in Springfield.

In 1842, it was in Springfield that Lincoln and his new bride, Mary Todd, bought the only house they would ever own and the place where three of their four sons were born. What's more, during his 1860 presidential campaign, Lincoln turned his Springfield home into his operating center for hosting strategy sessions, visiting delegations, and parades. Over the years since, Illinois politicians have told voters that legislators meeting at the capitol in Springfield get a strange feeling, a sense of Lincoln's spirit brooding above, to lead them to create ever better services for the people of his home state. I used to gather my Majic Bus students on the steps of the city capitol and give my lecture on Lincoln's Springfield years next to a bronze statue of the president who saved the Union. After all, the city does have a legitimate claim to Lincoln. But no matter how many colorful anecdotes I told, no matter how many of the town's historic markers we visited to study those sites' various events, it was always the trek to Lincoln's tomb that was the historical payoff and afterwards felt like an essential rite of passage for any American.

To prepare for the visit to Lincoln's tomb, I took my students first to 603 South Fifth Street, the house once owned by Lincoln's sister-in-law, which later became the lifelong home of Vachel Lindsay, whom critic Louis Untermeyer dubbed the greatest lyric poet since Edgar Allen Poe. Lindsay was born in the house in 1879 and committed suicide there in 1931, in between writing hundreds of memorable poems, mostly about the Midwest of the 1910s and '20s. Author Sinclair Lewis called him, "One of our few great poets, a power and a glory in the land."

It was while sitting on the porch of Lindsay's house that I read my students his haunting 1914 poem "Abraham Lincoln Walks at Midnight," verses that evoke the heavy heart of a man mourning in the rain over his son's grave and of a president alone at midnight in the White House after the Battle of Bull Run, begging God to help him end the Civil War. In Lindsay's poem Lincoln's ghost yet wanders the streets of Springfield, his spirit still a guiding force for our nation:

> *It is portentous, and a thing of state*
> *That here at midnight, in our little town*
> *A mourning figure walks, and will not rest,*
> *Near the old court-house pacing up and down,*
>
> *Or by his homestead, or in shadowed yards*
> *He lingers where his children used to play,*
> *Or through the market, on the well-worn stones*
> *He stalks until the dawn-stars burn away....*
>
> *It breaks his heart that kings must murder still,*
> *That all his hours of travail here for men*
> *Seem yet in vain. And who will bring white peace*
> *That he may sleep upon this hill again?*

From Lindsay's house, I traditionally instructed the Majic Bus driver to follow the same route as the procession of Lincoln's body in 1865, from the State Capitol to Oak Ridge Cemetery on the outskirts of town, where Lindsay is also buried. It was at Lincoln's gravesite that I told the students about his interment at which thousands of mourners heard prayers, sang hymns, and listened in tears as his inspirational second inaugural speech was read to them. The nation's grief was overwhelming, but only in Illinois was it said that the brown thrasher was not heard singing for an entire year after Lincoln was laid in his tomb.

But as Tennessee Williams put it in *A Streetcar Named Desire:* "Funerals are pretty compared with death." Over the years this has proved true via the various attempts that have been made to steal Lincoln's remains. In 1876 thieves with the idea of demanding $200,000 in ransom broke into Lincoln's tomb, forced open the sarcophagus, and pulled Lincoln's coffin partway out, but the would-be graverobbers were apprehended and each sentenced to a year in prison. Eventually, to prevent such desecration, Lincoln's body was reburied thirteen feet deep and surrounded by more than six feet of solid concrete.

A 117-foot obelisk towers over the granite tomb that houses the remains of Abraham Lincoln, his wife Mary Todd, and their sons—Edward, William, and Thomas; Robert, the eldest, is buried in Arlington National Cemetery. The family tomb's entrance is dominated by a bust of Lincoln as a beardless prairie lawyer designed by sculptor Larkin Mead and executed in bronze by Gutzon Borglum of Mount Rushmore fame. It is said that rubbing the bust's nose brings good luck, but after millions of visitors there's not much nose left. Inside the tomb, the walls are lined with passages from Lincoln speeches engraved in bronze, complementing a life-size statue of the president labeled *Great Emancipator*. A circular hallway leads to the marble burial chamber, where Secretary of War Edwin Stanton's famous reaction to Lincoln's death is literally etched in stone: "Now he belongs to the ages."

And so he does. The quiet of the horrific human toll of the Civil War —more than a half million Americans dead in their uniforms and many millions more suffering over their loss—has a heartbreaking immediacy. Pausing in the gloom where our sixteenth president lies almost mutes his ringing Gettysburg Address and the moral soaring of the Emancipation Proclamation beneath the echo of a line by poet Carl Sandburg: "When Abraham Lincoln was shoveled into the tombs, he forgot the copperheads and the assassin…in the dust, in the cool tombs." To most Americans, Lincoln's tomb is a melancholy shrine indeed—for as Harriet Beecher Stowe wrote in *Little Foxes* the year Lincoln died, "The bitterest tears shed over graves are for words left unsaid and deeds left undone."

Back then it was only after seeing the assassinated president's lanky body lying in a coffin that the American public realized in awe how unflappable he had stayed throughout those four years of civil terror. In his lifetime Lincoln had been belittled by many, even his friends mistaking his serenity for weakness. In death, however, his greatness became undeniable: seeing his remains returned in pomp to the common prairie soil, his citizens sobbed with the understanding that Lincoln had sacrificed himself for them and the nation. Under his stewardship all questions of division were settled: America was truly united and four million slaves freed. The collective recognition of the magnitude of these feats transformed Lincoln in retrospect into an American martyr for all time, a common man whose humility and forthrightness indeed forged a new nation. Sandburg once asked a railroad flagman to explain in just a few words why Lincoln was so beloved. Without hesitation the man replied: "He was humanity."

After we filed out of the cool vault, I usually asked my students to sit in front of the monument and jot their sentiments and reflections down in notebooks. There was something redemptive about visiting Lincoln's tomb in a group, the way there is in worshipping together with one's fellow man in church where all are temporarily free of earthly burdens. One former student, Jared Goldman, summed up the feeling nicely in his journal: "All around me is free air, free sight. Abraham Lincoln sought the freedom of all people. It is fitting for this site to give such a sense of freedom that I want to sing 'America the Beautiful. O beautiful for spacious skies.' I am here. This is America and more than just a place for the dead to lie. It is peace and freedom."

Strolling around the towering oaks through the gently rolling landscape of Oak Ridge Cemetery prompts a reconciliation with the past, a sense that the blood at Antietam and Shiloh and Gettysburg was not spilled in vain, that perhaps there is something to the myth that Lincoln was divinely sent to heal our nation by leading it undaunted through the divisive crisis over slavery that nearly tore it asunder.

But this sentiment fades in wandering past the headstones of the ordinary Americans who are also buried within the Oak Ridge Cemetery's lonely manicured grounds. There's something disturbing in the reflection that one will never know what Betty Potter or Jackson Lemmings did with their lives, whether they spent childhood in the Illinois backwoods or raised families in Chicago when it was just a hamlet. There may be more than 30,000 volumes on the Civil War in the Library of Congress alone, but nearly all the folks buried in the shadow of Abraham Lincoln's tomb will remain ever invisible to history. Yet they too played roles in our great national drama, and their ghosts also surely linger in Springfield at midnight alongside those of Lincoln and Lindsay.

In the end, however, cemeteries are for the living. Nearly all the dead presidents in *Who's Buried in Grant's Tomb?* are interred in imposing mausoleums, some with eternal flames kept lit in their honor. This is a fine tradition—provided it doesn't go too far. American presidents are not meant to be remembered with the grandeur accorded Egyptian pharaohs and French kings—our leaders rise not from royal pedigrees or dictatorial impulses but through hard work, patriotic conviction, and luck. Oak Ridge Cemetery is filled with Lindsay's "Lincoln-hearted," ordinary men and women with such an extraordinary belief in our great democratic experiment that it inspired them to build the United States into the strongest and freest nation in history. Thus it is that in some uniquely American way every grave at Oak Ridge seems as important as Lincoln's in a country where citizenship is the highest honor of all.

Some years ago, during a sojourn at Princeton University, I decided to stroll around the local cemetery to visit the grave of Grover Cleveland, the twenty-second and twenty-fourth president of the United States—the only chief executive to serve non-consecutive terms and the only Democrat elected to the White House between James Buchanan in 1856 and Woodrow Wilson in 1912. I had always felt a certain fondness toward Cleveland, whose political career was characterized by commonsense conservatism and honesty in governance. It surprised me, therefore, that as I searched Princeton Cemetery for Cleveland's grave I encountered not a single visitor there to pay their respects to this once towering political force. When I found the gravesite, I was further struck that there were no statues, no celebratory wreaths, no memorial bouquets of flowers—just a modest tombstone marking the resting place of the former president, his wife Frances, and their daughter Ruth. Textbook images of Grover Cleveland when he had served as the reformist mayor of Buffalo, New York, of when he took on the corruption of Tammany Hall, of how he handled the Pullman strike and the financial panic of 1893, flooded my brain in vain denial of the hard fact that this gigantic figure was no more than a pile of bones under the cold November ground of central New Jersey and had been for eighty years. Later, I came across something theologian Jonathan Edwards—who is also buried in Princeton Cemetery—wrote back in 1746 in his book *Procrastination*, "The bodies of those that made such a noise and tumult when alive, when dead, lie as quietly among the graves of their neighbors as any others."

Another long-ago quote rang true during my visit to Princeton Cemetery, where I also sought out the grave of one of the great anti-heroes in American history: onetime Vice President Aaron Burr, who is best remembered for killing former Treasury Secretary Alexander Hamilton in an 1804 pistol duel. But as I stood at his gravesite instead of feeling animosity toward Burr, I was engulfed by an unexpected wave of compassion. I understood what Washington Irving had meant in 1820 when he wrote in *The Sketch Book*: "Who can look down upon the grave even of an enemy, and not feel a compunctious throb, that he should ever have warred with the poor handful of earth that lies mouldering before him."

Cemeteries are some of the least appreciated, even most mocked, public spaces in America. Thus, when Brian Lamb first told me of his plan to write a book on presidential gravesites, I knew he would be in for a round of ridicule. After all, in 1948 supremely snide British writer Evelyn Waugh devoted an entire novel, *The Loved One*, to lampooning California's famous Forest Lawn, barely disguised as Whispering Glades Memorial Park.

Waugh's acetose satire of American cemeteries was published just a few years after his countryman Aldous Huxley's novel *After Many a Summer Dies the Swan*, which also made sport of the promise of immortality that cemeteries like Forest Lawn were selling. Waugh and Huxley derided the "memorial park" as a harmful illusion designed to mask the reality of death, thus denying its purpose in society. In his 1947 *Life* magazine article "Death in Hollywood," Waugh averred that death should remind "a highly civilized people that beauty [is] skin deep and pomp mortal." He would not have thought much, it seems, of President John F. Kennedy's eternal flame at Arlington National Cemetery. Rather, Waugh argued that at the Forest Lawns of America the body is not allowed to decay: instead, "it lives on, more chic in death than ever before, in its indestructible Class A steel-and-concrete shelf; the soul goes straight from the Slumber Room to Paradise, where it enjoys an endless infancy."

One suspects that neither my Majic Bus visit to Lincoln's grave nor Brian Lamb's *Who's Buried in Grant's Tomb?* are the sort of enterprises of which Waugh and Huxley would have approved, sniffing as they would at the study of presidents' deaths as an exercise in morbid triviality. But they were a couple of Anglocentric snobs feeding off California's golden riches even while mocking the American way of doing everything, including death. Had they ever deigned to visit Ohio, how they would have snickered at the imposing Harding Tomb in Marion or the gargantuan McKinley Mausoleum in Canton—such ridiculous and meaningless sites. But what those blinded by cynicism fail to understand is that the purpose of a visit to, say, James Madison's grave at Virginia's Montpelier Station is not the mawkish worship of a founding father. No, a pilgrimage to a president's grave is instead a way to pay quiet tribute to all of our glorious past, to thank the militiamen who lost their lives at Bunker Hill, to honor the oratory of Patrick Henry, to salute the valor of the men who died at Iwo Jima and Midway and a hundred other flyspeck islands in the Pacific. All presidents—no matter how well they performed in office—are revered by most Americans simply because they represent our grandest political traditions.

Ever since first president George Washington died on December 14, 1799, the United States has looked to its leaders' funerals as a means to unite the nation. Partisan bickering is put in check, flags are flown at half-staff, and solo trumpeters blow taps from the Jefferson Memorial to Mt. McKinley. The death of a president is a time of collective mourning and national pulse-taking, a yardstick moment to reflect how far we've come and how much remains to be done before America truly becomes Massachusetts colonist John Winthrop's "city upon a hill."

As a quintessential American and a Hoosier who regularly strolls the grounds of Crown Hill Cemetery in Indianapolis, where twenty-third president Benjamin Harrison is buried, C-SPAN founder Brian Lamb understands how presidents' graves serve as guideposts to our past and why a moment of quiet reflection in such places nourishes the soul and fuels the historical imagination. It's a way to make a connection with the lives of the individuals who helped shape our nation.

Lamb's attraction to presidential burial sites does not arise from some odd fascination with entombment; he is not the least thanatophilic and has as healthy a fear of death as anyone. His interest is instead that of a serious student of American history who simply has come to learn that both the lives and deaths of presidents play a part in our national drama. After all, the deaths of Washington, Jefferson, Adams, Lincoln, FDR, and JFK surely rank among the most memorable days in American history.

Detailing these events makes an intriguing read as well as a useful reference work in the form of a guidebook that encourages the traveler to put historical cemeteries on their itineraries. More recent presidents including Herbert Hoover, Franklin Roosevelt, Dwight Eisenhower, and Richard Nixon are buried on the grounds of their respective presidential libraries, so their graves are just the capstone on an afternoon of learning. There is an added value to Arlington National Cemetery as well; in addition to John F. Kennedy's tomb with its eternal flame, visitors can also pause at the final resting places of such diverse patriots as Omar Bradley, Medgar Evers, Oliver Wendell Holmes, George Marshall, William Howard Taft, and Earl Warren. And when we ponder all those endless rows of white crosses marking how many of our forebears lost their lives fighting for our freedom, we can't help but be moved.

Enlightenment can be found at every presidential grave. It doesn't matter what the various polls say about a past president's rank by order of greatness, a consensus that usually puts Washington, Jefferson, Lincoln, and both Roosevelts at the top, with the likes of Hoover, Harding, and Nixon at the bottom.

What makes *Who's Buried in Grant's Tomb?* so refreshing is its avoidance of this poll-driven approach, instead giving all our past presidents equal billing in death; the chapter on Franklin Pierce is thus nearly as long as the one on Franklin Roosevelt. Of course, this egalitarianism will come as no surprise to C-SPAN viewers familiar with the network's dispassionate, straight-down-the-middle style. In this book, refraining from favoritism allows C-SPAN to pay homage to the *institution* of the presidency and not just to the extraordinary individuals who have staffed it.

And the folks at C-SPAN are right: visiting any one of the presidents' gravesites provides just as perfect an opportunity to meditate on the Constitution and the Bill of Rights, on slavery and emancipation, on agrarianism and industrialism—on any event, large or small, that ever contributed to the forging of our nation. For great thoughts are inspired by contemplating the lives of great men, and every American president has been great in having the supreme courage to take on the job. As Theodore

Roosevelt declared in an often quoted speech at the Sorbonne in Paris on April 23, 1910, "It is not the critic who counts, not the man who points out how the strong man stumbles, or where the doer of deeds could have done better. The credit belongs to the man who is actually in the arena; whose face is marred by dust and sweat and blood...."

After all, the White House is the zenith of American ambition, attained by only a rare few of those bold enough to seek it. By succeeding in the highest arena, our presidents have earned their places as what Ralph Waldo Emerson called "inextinguishable beings."

Shortly after the death of Abraham Lincoln, Henry Ward Beecher, pastor of Brooklyn, New York's Plymouth Church, echoed Emerson's distinction in a sermon on the newly filled tomb in Springfield. "Four years ago, O' Illinois, we took from your midst an untried man and from among the people," Beecher intoned. "We return him to you a mighty conqueror. Not thine any more, but the nation's; not ours but the world's. Give him place, O' ye prairies. In the midst of this great continent his dust shall rest, a sacred treasure to myriads who shall pilgrim to that shrine to kindle anew their zeal and patriotism."

Due to 24/7 TV coverage of presidential funerals, the recent deaths of Ronald Reagan and Gerald Ford have become coronations. Anybody who ever shook hands with Reagan or Ford became a prime interview candidate. For both men, long film tribute biographies were aired over and over again on the networks. Reagan and Ford were honored more in death than in life. The joke, "Who's buried in Grant's tomb?" just doesn't work anymore; the new parlor room game by the year 2000 was what major American politician *wasn't* at the presidential memorial service. In death, modern U.S. presidents are guaranteed to get an upward revision by the general public. They are our own version of royalty. And the presidential tombs are routinely visited by school groups and campers, curiosity seekers and scholars, tourists and wanderers. Onlookers pause, if only for a moment, to pay private homage at the graves of the bold, often flawed men who have led our nation. Somehow at these final presidential resting places the pageant of democracy flourishes.

Remember me as you pass by

As you are now, so once was I,

As I am now so you must be

Prepare for death and follow me.

—Traditional epitaph

Appendices

Presidents Who Died in Office

President	Date of Death	Place of Death
William Henry Harrison	April 4, 1841	Washington, D.C.
Zachary Taylor	July 9, 1850	Washington, D.C.
Abraham Lincoln (assassinated)	April 15, 1865	Washington, D.C.
James Garfield (assassinated)	September 19, 1881	Elberon, New Jersey
William McKinley (assassinated)	September 14, 1901	Buffalo, New York
Warren G. Harding	August 2, 1923	San Francisco, California
Franklin Delano Roosevelt	April 12, 1945	Warm Springs, Georgia
John F. Kennedy (assassinated)	November 22, 1963	Dallas, Texas

Source: *Presidential Fact Book*

Presidents' Length of Retirement after Leaving Office

President	Retirement
James K. Polk	103 days
Chester A. Arthur	1 year, 260 days
George Washington	2 years, 285 days
Woodrow Wilson	2 years, 337 days
Calvin Coolidge	3 years, 308 days
Lyndon Baines Johnson	4 years, 2 days
James Monroe	6 years, 122 days
Andrew Johnson	6 years, 149 days
James Buchanan	7 years, 89 days
Benjamin Harrison	8 years, 9 days
Dwight D. Eisenhower	8 years, 67 days
Andrew Jackson	8 years, 96 days
Ulysses S. Grant	8 years, 141 days
Theodore Roosevelt	9 years, 309 days
Grover Cleveland	11 years, 112 days (after second term)
Rutherford B. Hayes	11 years, 319 days
Franklin Pierce	12 years, 218 days
John Tyler	16 years, 320 days
William Howard Taft	17 years, 4 days
Thomas Jefferson	17 years, 122 days

John Quincy Adams. . . . . 18 years, 356 days

James Madison. . . . . 19 years, 116 days

Richard Nixon . . . . 19 years, 256 days

Harry S. Truman . . . . 19 years, 340 days

Millard Fillmore. . . . . 21 years, 4 days

Martin Van Buren . . . . 21 years, 142 days

John Adams . . . . 25 years, 122 days

Herbert Hoover. . . . . 31 years, 231 days

Gerald R. Ford. . . . . 29 years, 342 days

Jimmy Carter . . . . ———

Ronald Reagan. . . . . 15 years, 137 days

George Bush. . . . . ———

William Jefferson Clinton . . . . ———

George W. Bush. . . . . ———

Barack Obama . . . . ———

Source: *Presidential Fact Book*

Appendix B   **218**

Presidents and Their Wives: Dates of Death and Places of Burial

George Washington

December 14, 1799; 67 years, 295 days; Mount Vernon Estate, Mount Vernon, Virginia

Martha Custis Washington

May 22, 1802; 70 years, 335 days; Mount Vernon Estate, Mount Vernon, Virginia

John Adams

July 4, 1826; 90 years, 247 days; United First Parish Church, Quincy, Massachusetts

Abigail Smith Adams

October 28, 1818; 73 years, 351 days; United First Parish Church, Quincy, Massachusetts

Thomas Jefferson

July 4, 1826; 83 years, 82 days; Monticello, Charlottesville, Virginia

Martha Skelton Jefferson

September 6, 1782; 33 years, 322 days; Monticello, Charlottesville, Virginia

James Madison

June 28, 1836; 85 years, 104 days; Montpelier Estate, Montpelier Station, Virginia

Dolley Madison

July 12, 1849; 81 years, 53 days; Montpelier Estate, Montpelier Station, Virginia

James Monroe

July 4, 1831; 73 years, 67 days; Hollywood Cemetery, Richmond, Virginia

Elizabeth Kortright Monroe

September 23, 1830; 62 years, 85 days; Hollywood Cemetery, Richmond, Virginia

John Quincy Adams

February 23, 1848; 80 years, 227 days; United First Parish Church, Quincy, Massachusetts

Louisa Catherine Johnson Adams

May 14, 1852; 77 years, 91 days; United First Parish Church, Quincy, Massachusetts

Andrew Jackson

June 8, 1845; 78 years, 85 days; The Hermitage, Hermitage, Tennessee

Rachel Donelson Robards Jackson

December 22, 1828; 61 years, 190 days; The Hermitage, Hermitage, Tennessee

Martin Van Buren

July 24, 1862; 79 years, 231 days; Kinderhook Reformed Cemetery, Kinderhook, New York

Hannah Hoes Van Buren

February 5, 1819; 35 years, 334 days; Kinderhook Reformed Cemetery, Kinderhook, New York

William Henry Harrison
April 4, 1841; 68 years, 54 days; Harrison Tomb, North Bend, Ohio

Anna Tuthill Symmes Harrison
February 25, 1864; 88 years, 215 days; Harrison Tomb, North Bend, Ohio

John Tyler
January 18, 1862; 71 years, 295 days; Hollywood Cemetery, Richmond, Virginia

1st Wife: Letitia Christian Tyler
September 10, 1842; 51 years, 302 days; Cedar Grove, New Kent County, Virginia

2nd Wife: Julia Gardiner Tyler
July 10, 1889; 69 years, 67 days; Hollywood Cemetery, Richmond, Virginia

James K. Polk
June 15, 1849; 53 years, 225 days; State Capitol, Nashville, Tennessee

Sarah Childress Polk
August 14, 1891; 87 years, 344 days; State Capitol, Nashville, Tennessee

Zachary Taylor
July 9, 1850; 65 years, 227 days; Zachary Taylor National Cemetery, Louisville, Kentucky

Margaret Mackall Smith Taylor
August 18, 1852; 63 years, 331 days; Zachary Taylor National Cemetery, Louisville, Kentucky

Millard Fillmore
March 8, 1874; 74 years, 60 days; Forest Lawn Cemetery, Buffalo, New York

1st Wife: Abigail Powers Fillmore
March 30, 1853; 55 years, 17 days; Forest Lawn Cemetery, Buffalo, New York

2nd Wife: Caroline Carmichael McIntosh Fillmore
August 11, 1881; 67 years, 294 days; Forest Lawn Cemetery, Buffalo, New York

Franklin Pierce

October 8, 1869; 64 years, 319 days; Old North Cemetery, Concord, New Hampshire

Jane Means Appleton Pierce

December 2,1863; 57 years, 265 days; Old North Cemetery, Concord, New Hampshire

James Buchanan

June 1, 1868; 77 years, 40 days; Woodward Hill Cemetery, Lancaster, Pennsylvania

Abraham Lincoln

April 15, 1865; 56 years, 62 days; Oak Ridge Cemetery, Springfield, Illinois

Mary Todd Lincoln

July 16, 1882: 63 years, 215 days; Oak Ridge Cemetery, Springfield, Illinois

Andrew Johnson

July 31, 1875; 66 years, 214 days; Andrew Johnson National Cemetery, Greeneville, Tennessee

Eliza McCardle Johnson

January 15, 1876; 65 years, 103 days; Andrew Johnson National Cemetery, Greeneville, Tennessee

Ulysses S. Grant

July 23, 1885; 63 years, 87 days; General Grant National Memorial, New York, New York

Julia Boggs Dent Grant

December 14, 1902; 76 years, 322 days; General Grant National Memorial, New York, New York

Rutherford B. Hayes

January 17, 1893; 70 years, 105 days; Hayes Presidential Center, Fremont, Ohio

Lucy Ware Webb Hayes

June 25, 1889; 57 years, 301 days; Hayes Presidential Center, Fremont, Ohio

James Garfield

September 19, 1881; 49 years, 304 days; Lake View Cemetery, Cleveland, Ohio

Lucretia Rudolph Garfield

March 14, 1918; 85 years, 329 days; Lake View Cemetery, Cleveland, Ohio

Chester Arthur

November 18, 1886; 57 years, 44 days; Albany Rural Cemetery, Albany, New York

Ellen Herndon Arthur

January 12, 1880; 42 years, 135 days; Albany Rural Cemetery, Albany, New York

Grover Cleveland

June 24, 1908; 71 years, 98 days; Princeton Cemetery, Princeton, New Jersey

Frances Folsom Cleveland

October 29, 1947; 83 years, 100 days; Princeton Cemetery, Princeton, New Jersey

Benjamin Harrison

March 13, 1901; 67 years, 205 days; Crown Hill Cemetery, Indianapolis, Indiana

1st Wife: Caroline Lavinia Scott Harrison

October 25, 1892; 60 years, 24 days; Crown Hill Cemetery, Indianapolis, Indiana

2nd Wife: Mary Lord Dimmick Harrison

January 5, 1948; 89 years, 250 days; Crown Hill Cemetery, Indianapolis, Indiana

William McKinley

September 14, 1901; 58 years, 228 days; McKinley National Memorial and Museum, Canton, Ohio

Ida Saxton McKinley

May 26, 1907; 59 years, 352 days; McKinley National Memorial and Museum, Canton, Ohio

Theodore Roosevelt

January 6, 1919; 60 years, 71 days; Young's Memorial Cemetery, Oyster Bay, New York

1st Wife: Alice Hathaway Lee Roosevelt

February 14, 1884; 22 years, 192 days; Greenwood Cemetery, Cambridge, Massachusetts

2nd Wife: Edith Carow Roosevelt

September 30, 1948; 87 years, 45 days; Young's Memorial Cemetery, Oyster Bay, New York

William Howard Taft

March 8, 1930; 72 years, 174 days; Arlington National Cemetery, Arlington, Virginia

Helen Herron Taft

May 22, 1943; 82 years, 140 days; Arlington National Cemetery, Arlington, Virginia

Woodrow Wilson

February 3, 1924; 67 years, 36 days; Washington National Cathedral, Washington, D.C.

1st Wife: Ellen Louise Axson Wilson

August 6, 1914; 54 years, 83 days; Myrtle Hill Cemetery, Rome, Georgia

2nd Wife: Edith Bolling Galt Wilson

December 28, 1961; 89 years, 64 days; Washington National Cathedral, Washington, D.C.

Warren G. Harding

August 2, 1923; 57 years, 273 days; Harding Tomb, Marion, Ohio

Florence Kling Harding

November 21, 1924; 64 years, 98 days; Harding Tomb, Marion, Ohio

Calvin Coolidge

January 5, 1933; 60 years, 185 days; Plymouth Cemetery, Plymouth, Vermont

Grace Anna Goodhue Coolidge

July 8, 1957; 78 years, 186 days; Plymouth Cemetery, Plymouth, Vermont

Herbert Hoover

October 20, 1964; 90 years, 71 days; Herbert Hoover Library and Birthplace, West Branch, Iowa

Lou Henry Hoover

January 7, 1944; 69 years, 284 days; Herbert Hoover Library and Birthplace, West Branch, Iowa

Franklin Delano Roosevelt

April 12, 1945; 63 years, 72 days; Franklin Roosevelt Library and Museum, Hyde Park, New York

Eleanor Roosevelt

November 7, 1962; 78 years, 27 days; Franklin Roosevelt Library and Museum, Hyde Park, New York

Harry S. Truman

December 26, 1972; 88 years, 232 days; Harry S. Truman Library, Independence, Missouri

Elizabeth "Bess" Virginia Wallace Truman

October 18, 1982; 97 years, 247 days; Harry S. Truman Library, Independence, Missouri

Dwight D. Eisenhower

March 28, 1969; 78 years, 165 days; Dwight D. Eisenhower Library and Museum, Abilene, Kansas

Marie "Mamie" Genevea Doud Eisenhower

November 1, 1979; 82 years, 352 days; Dwight D. Eisenhower Library and Museum, Abilene, Kansas

John F. Kennedy

November 22, 1963; 46 years, 177 days; Arlington National Cemetery, Arlington, Virginia

Jacqueline Lee Bouvier Kennedy Onassis

May 19, 1994; 64 years, 295 days; Arlington National Cemetery, Arlington, Virginia

Lyndon Baines Johnson

January 22, 1973; 64 years, 148 days; LBJ Ranch, Johnson City, Texas

Claudia Alta "Lady Bird" Johnson

July 11, 2007; 94 years, 202 days; LBJ Ranch, Johnson City, Texas

Richard Nixon

April 22, 1994; 81 years, 104 days; Richard Nixon Library and Birthplace, Yorba Linda, California

Patricia Ryan Nixon

June 22, 1993; 81 years, 98 days; Richard Nixon Library and Birthplace, Yorba Linda, California

Gerald Ford

December 26, 2006; 93 years, 165 days; Gerald R. Ford Presidential Museum, Grand Rapids, Michigan

Elizabeth "Betty" Bloomer Ford—

Jimmy Carter—

Rosalynn Smith Carter—

Ronald Reagan

June 5, 2004; 93 years, 120 days; Ronald Reagan Presidential Library, Simi Valley, California

1st Wife: Jane Wyman

September 10, 2007; 90 years, 248 days; Forest Lawn Cemetery, Cathedral City, California

2nd Wife: Nancy Davis Reagan—

George Bush—

Barbara Pierce Bush—

William Jefferson Clinton—

Hillary Rodham Clinton—

George W. Bush—

Laura Welch Bush—

Barack Obama—

Michelle Robinson Obama—

Vice Presidents and Their Gravesites

Administration	Vice President
Washington 1789–1797	1. John Adams, Federalist Buried: United First Parish Church 1306 Hancock St., Quincy, MA (617) 773–1290; www.ufpc.org
J. Adams 1797–1801	2. Thomas Jefferson, Democratic-Republican Buried: Monticello Virginia Highway/Thomas Jefferson Parkway, Charlottesville, VA (804) 984–9822; www.monticello.org
Jefferson 1801–1805	3. Aaron Burr, Democratic-Republican Buried: Princeton Cemetery 29 Greenview Ave., Princeton, NJ (609) 924–1369 www.princetonol.com/patron/cemetery.html

1805–1809	4. George Clinton, Democratic-Republican
	Buried: Old Dutch Churchyard
	272 Wall St., Kingston, NY
	(845) 338–6759
	www.ci.kingston.ny.us/tourism/
	museums.html

Madison

1809–1812	4. George Clinton, Democratic-Republican
	See above.
1813–1814	5. Elbridge Gerry, Democratic-Republican
	Buried: Congressional Cemetery
	1801 E St. SE, Washington, DC
	(202) 543–0539
	www.congressionalcemetery.org/
1814–1817	*No vice president.*

Monroe

1817–1825	6. Daniel D. Tompkins, Democratic-Republican
	Buried: St. Mark's Church-in-the-Bowery
	131 E. 10th St., New York City, NY
	(212) 674–6377
	www.saintmarkschurch.org

J.Q. Adams

1825–1829	7. John C. Calhoun, Democratic-Republican
	Buried: St. Philip's Episcopal Church
	146 Church St., Charleston, SC
	(843) 722–7734
	www.stphilipschurchsc.org

Jackson

1829–1832

7. John C. Calhoun, Democratic-
Republican
See above.

1833–1837

8. Martin Van Buren, Democrat
Buried: Kinderhook Reformed
Cemetery
Albany Avenue, Kinderhook, NY
(518) 758–9689
www.kinderhookconnection.com/
history.htm

Van Buren

1837–1841

9. Richard M. Johnson, Democrat
Buried: Frankfort Cemetery
215 E. Main St., Frankfort, KY
(502) 227–2403
www.visitfrankfort.com/points/
boonegrave.html

W.H. Harrison

1841

10. John Tyler, Whig
Buried: Hollywood Cemetery
412 S. Cherry St., Richmond, VA
(804) 648–8501
www.hollywoodcemetery.org

Tyler

1841–1845

No vice president.

Polk

1845–1849

11. George M. Dallas, Democrat
Buried: St. Peter's Churchyard
313 Pine St., Philadelphia, PA
(215) 925–5968; www.stpetersphila.org

Taylor
1849–1850

12. Millard Fillmore, Whig
Buried: Forest Lawn Cemetery
1411 Delaware Ave., Buffalo, NY
(716) 885–1600; www.forest-lawn.com

Fillmore
1850–1853

No vice president.

Pierce
1853

13. William R. King, Democrat
Buried: Live Oak Cemetery
Dallas Avenue and King Street,
Selma, AL
(334) 874–2160
www.selmaalabama.com/attract.htm

1853–1857

No vice president.

Buchanan
1857–1861

14. John C. Breckinridge, Democrat
Buried: Lexington National Cemetery
833 W. Main St., Lexington, KY
(859) 885–5727;
www.cem.va.gov/pdf/lexington.pdf

Lincoln
1861–1865

15. Hannibal Hamlin, Republican
Buried: Mt. Hope Cemetery
1048 State St., Bangor, ME
(207) 945–6589; www.mthopebgr.com

1865

16. Andrew Johnson, Republican
Buried: Andrew Johnson National
Cemetery
121 Monument Ave., Greeneville, TN
(423) 638–3551; www.nps.gov/anjo

A. Johnson
1865–1869   *No vice president.*

Grant
1869–1873   17. Schuyler Colfax, Republican
                                   Buried: City Cemetery
                                   214 Elm St., South Bend, IN
                                   (574) 235–9458
1873–1875   18. Henry Wilson, Republican
                                   Buried: Old Dell Park Cemetery
                                   163 Pond St., Natick, MA
                                   (508) 655–1271
1875–1877   *No vice president.*

Hayes
1877–1881   19. William A. Wheeler, Republican
                                   Buried: Morningside Cemetery
                                   Raymond Street, Malone, NY

Garfield
1881   20. Chester A. Arthur, Republican
                                   Buried: Albany Rural Cemetery
                                   Cemetery Avenue, Menands, NY
                                   (518) 463–7017

Arthur
1881–1885   *No vice president.*

Cleveland
1885   21. Thomas A. Hendricks, Democrat
                                   Buried: Crown Hill Cemetery
                                   700 W. 38th St., Indianapolis, IN
                                   (317) 925–8231; www.crownhill.org
1885–1889   *No vice president.*

B. Harrison
1889–1893

22. Levi P. Morton, Republican
Buried: Rhinebeck Cemetery
3 Mill Road, Rhinebeck, NY
(845) 876–3961

Cleveland
1893–1897

23. Adlai E. Stevenson, Democrat
Buried: Evergreen Cemetery
302 E. Miller St., Bloomington, IL
(309) 827–6950
www.evergreen-cemetery.com

McKinley
1897–1899

24. Garret A. Hobart, Republican
Buried: Cedar Lawn Cemetery
McLean Blvd. and Crooks Ave.,
Paterson, NJ
(973) 279–1161

1901

25. Theodore Roosevelt, Republican
Buried: Young's Memorial Cemetery
Cove Road, Oyster Bay, NY
(516) 922–4788; www.nps.gov/sahi/

T. Roosevelt
1901–1905

No vice president.

1905–1909

26. Charles W. Fairbanks, Republican
Buried: Crown Hill Cemetery
700 W. 38th St., Indianapolis, IN
(317) 925–8231; www.crownhill.org

Taft
1909–1912

27. James S. Sherman, Republican
Buried: Forest Hill Cemetery
2201 Oneida St., Utica, NY
(315) 735–2701
vintageviews.org/vvny/UZ/cards/
u001.html

Wilson
1913–1921

28. Thomas R. Marshall, Democrat
Buried: Crown Hill Cemetery
700 W. 38th St., Indianapolis, IN
(317) 925–8231; www.crownhill.org

Harding
1921–1923

29. Calvin Coolidge, Republican
Buried: Plymouth Notch Cemetery
Vermont Highway 100A, Plymouth, VT
(802) 672–3773
www.historicvermont.org/html/
CoolidgeTour.html

Coolidge
1923–1925
1925–1929

No vice president.
30. Charles G. Dawes, Republican
Buried: Rosehill Cemetery
5800 N. Ravenswood Ave., Chicago, IL
(773) 561–5940
www.graveyeards.com/rosehill

Hoover
1929–1933

31. Charles Curtis, Republican
Buried: Topeka Cemetery
1601 E. 10th St., Topeka, KS
(785) 233–4132

F. Roosevelt
1933–1941

32. John N. Garner, Democrat
Buried: Uvalde Cemetery
U.S. Highway 90 West, Uvalde, TX
(830) 278–5018

1941–1945	33. Henry A. Wallace, Democrat
	Buried: Glendale Cemetery
	4909 University Ave., Des Moines, IA
	(515) 271–8722
1945	34. Harry S. Truman, Democrat
	Buried: Harry S. Truman Library
	U.S. Highway 24 at Delaware Street,
	Independence, MO
	(800) 833–1225
	www.trumanlibrary.org

Truman
1945–1949	*No vice president.*
1949–1953	35. Alben W. Barkley, Democrat
	Buried: Mt. Kenton Cemetery
	Lone Oak Road, U.S. Highway 45
	South, Paducah, KY
	(270) 554–1566
	www2.apex.net/users/firstpres/
	mtkenton.html

Eisenhower
1953–1961	36. Richard M. Nixon, Republican
	Buried: Richard Nixon Library and
	Birthplace
	18001 Yorba Linda Blvd., Yorba Linda,
	CA
	(714) 993–5075
	www.nixonfoundation.org

Kennedy
1961–1963

37. Lyndon Baines Johnson, Democrat
Buried: LBJ Ranch
U.S. Highway 290, Johnson City, TX
(830) 868–7128
www.nps.gov/lyjo/cem.htm

L. Johnson
1963–1965

No vice president.

1965–1969

38. Hubert H. Humphrey, Democrat
Buried: Lakewood Cemetery
3600 Hennepin Ave., Minneapolis, MN
(612) 822–2171
www.lakewoodcemetery.com

Nixon
1969–1973

39. Spiro T. Agnew, Republican
Buried: Dulaney Valley Memorial
Gardens
200 Padonia Rd. East, Timonium, MD
(410) 666–0490
www.dulaneyvalley.com

1973–1974

40. Gerald R. Ford, Republican
Buried: Ford Presidential Museum
303 Pearl St., NW, Grand Rapids, MI
(616) 254–0400
www.fordlibrarymuseum.gov

Ford
1974–1977

41. Nelson Rockefeller, Republican
Buried: Sleepy Hollow Cemetery
U.S. Highway 9, Sleepy Hollow, NY
(plot not open to public, though rest
of cemetery is open)
(914) 631–9491

Carter
1977–1981   42. Walter Mondale, Democrat

Reagan
1981–1989   43. George H.W. Bush, Republican

G.H.W. Bush
1989–1993   44. J. Danforth Quayle, Republican

Clinton
1993–2001   45. Albert A. Gore Jr., Democrat

G.W. Bush
2001–2009   46. Richard B. Cheney, Republican

Obama
2009–   47. Joseph R. Biden Jr., Democrat

Presidential and Vice Presidential Gravesites by State

New York
Martin Van Buren: P, VP

Millard Fillmore: P, VP

Ulysses S. Grant: P

Chester Arthur: P, VP

Theodore Roosevelt: P, VP

Franklin Delano Roosevelt: P

George Clinton: VP

Daniel D. Tompkins: VP

William A. Wheeler: VP

Levi P. Morton: VP

James S. Sherman: VP

Nelson A. Rockefeller: VP

Virginia
George Washington: P

Thomas Jefferson: P, VP

James Madison: P

James Monroe: P

John Tyler: P, VP

William Howard Taft: P

John F. Kennedy: P

Indiana

Benjamin Harrison: P
Schuyler Colfax: VP
Thomas A. Hendricks: VP
Charles W. Fairbanks: VP
Thomas R. Marshall: VP

Kentucky

Zachary Taylor: P
Richard M. Johnson: VP
John C. Breckinridge: VP
Alben W. Barkley: VP

Ohio

William Henry Harrison: P
Rutherford B. Hayes: P
James Garfield: P
William McKinley: P
Warren G. Harding: P

New Jersey

Grover Cleveland: P
Aaron Burr: VP
Garret A. Hobart: VP

Massachusetts

John Adams: P, VP
John Quincy Adams: P
Henry Wilson: VP

Tennessee

Andrew Jackson: P
James K. Polk: P
Andrew Johnson: P, VP

Illinois
Abraham Lincoln: P
Charles G. Dawes: VP
Adlai E. Stevenson: VP

California
Richard Nixon: P, VP
Ronald Reagan: P

Iowa
Herbert Hoover: P
Henry A. Wallace: VP

Kansas
Dwight D. Eisenhower: P
Charles Curtis: VP

Pennsylvania
James Buchanan: P
George M. Dallas: VP

Texas
Lyndon Baines Johnson: P, VP
John Nance Garner: VP

Washington, D.C.
Woodrow Wilson: P
Elbridge Gerry: VP

Alabama
William R. King: VP

Maine
Hannibal Hamlin: VP

Maryland
Spiro T. Agnew: VP

Appendix E

Michigan
Gerald Ford: P, VP

Minnesota
Hubert H. Humphrey: VP

Missouri
Harry S. Truman: P, VP

New Hampshire
Franklin Pierce: P

South Carolina
John C. Calhoun: VP

Vermont
Calvin Coolidge: P, VP

Presidential Libraries

Concerned about the number of papers generated during his term in office, Franklin D. Roosevelt came up with the idea of establishing a presidential library to be administered by the National Archives. Today ten presidential libraries are run through the National Archives. The three exceptions are the Rutherford B. Hayes Presidential Center, which opened in 1916, the Abraham Lincoln Presidential Library, which is administered by the Illinois Historic Preservation Agency, and the Richard Nixon Library and Birthplace which is privately held; Nixon's papers are at the National Archives in College Park, Maryland.

Presidential Library	Estimated Annual Visitors
Abraham Lincoln Presidential Library	400,000

scheduled to open in November, 2002
112 N. 6th St., Springfield, IL 62701
(800)610–2094, (217) 782–5674; www.alincoln-library.com

Rutherford B. Hayes Presidential Center	50,000

Spiegel Grove, Fremont, OH 43420
(800)998-7737; www.rbhayes.org

Herbert Hoover Presidential Library and Museum	52,000

210 Parkside Dr., PO Box 488, West Branch, IA 52358
(319) 643-5301; www.hoover.nara.gov

Presidential Library	Estimated Annual Visitors

Franklin D. Roosevelt Library and Museum   113,000
4079 Albany Post Rd., Hyde Park, NY 12538
(845) 486-7700; www.fdrlibrary.marist.edu

Harry S. Truman Library   100,000
500 West U.S. Highway 24, Independence, MO 64050
(800)833-1225; www.trumanlibrary.org

Dwight D. Eisenhower Library and Museum   70,000
200 SE 4th St., Abilene, KS 67410
(785)263-4751; www.eisenhower.archives.gov

John F. Kennedy Presidential Library and Museum   212,000
Columbia Point, Boston, MA 02125
(866)JFK-1960; www.jfklibrary.org

Lyndon B. Johnson Library   257,813
2313 Red River St., Austin, TX 78705
(512)721-0200; www.lbjlib.utexas.edu

Richard Nixon Library and Birthplace   131,522
18001 Yorba Linda Blvd., Yorba Linda, CA 92886
(714)993-5075; www.nixonfoundation.org

Gerald R. Ford Museum   110,000
303 Pearl St. NW, Grand Rapids, MI 49504
(616)254-0400; www.ford.utexas.edu

Gerald R. Ford Library   4,000
1000 Beal Ave., Ann Arbor, MI 48109
(734)205-0555; www.ford.utexas.edu

The Jimmy Carter Presidential Library and Museum   47,374
441 Freedom Pkwy., Atlanta, GA 30307
(404)865-7100; www.jimmycarterlibrary.org

The Ronald Reagan Presidential Library and Museum   **380,000**
40 Presidential Dr., Simi Valley, CA 93065
(800)410-8354; www.reagan.utexas.edu

The George Bush Presidential Library and Museum   **150,000**
1000 George Bush Dr. West, College Station, TX 77845
(979)691-4000; www.bushlibrary.tamu.edu

William J. Clinton Presidential Library and Museum   **N/A**
1200 President Clinton Ave., Little Rock, AR 72201
(501)374-4242; www.clintonlibrary.gov

Estimated annual visitors based on 2008 numbers.

For additional information:
Office of Presidential Libraries, National Archives
and Records Administration
700 Pennsylvania Ave., NW, Washington, DC 20408
(866) 325-7208; www.nara.gov

Numbers for estimated annual visitors supplied by each library/museum.

Bibliography

DeGregorio, William A. *The Complete Book of U.S. Presidents.* New York, NY. Wings Books, 1984.

Donald, David Herbert. *Lincoln.* New York, NY. Simon & Schuster, 1995.

Ellis, Joseph. *Passionate Sage: The Character and Legacy of John Adams.* New York, NY. W.W. Norton, 1993.

Goodwin, Doris Kearns. *No Ordinary Time.* New York, NY. Simon & Schuster, 1994.

Heckscher, August. *Woodrow Wilson: A Biography.* New York, NY. Scribner's, 1991.

Kane, Joseph Nathan. *Presidential Fact Book.* New York, NY. Random House, 1998.

Klein, Philip Shriver. *President James Buchanan.* State College, PA. Pennsylvania State University Press, 1962.

Lord, Walter. *The Good Years: 1900-1914.* New York, NY. Harper & Row, 1960.

Manchester, William. *The Death of a President.* New York, NY. Harper & Row, 1967.

McCullough, David. *Truman.* New York, NY. Simon & Schuster, 1992.

Miller, Nathan. *Theodore Roosevelt: A Life.* New York, NY. William Morrow, 1992.

Nagel, Paul C. *John Quincy Adams: A Public Life, a Private Life.* New York, NY. Alfred A. Knopf, 1997.

Nichols, Roy Franklin. *Franklin Pierce: Young Hickory of the Granite Hills.* Norwalk, CT. Easton Press, 1969.

Raback, Robert J. *Millard Fillmore: Biography of a President.* Norwalk, CT. Easton Press, 1959.

Smith, Richard Norton. *Patriarch: George Washington and the New American Nation.* Boston, MA. Houghton Mifflin, 1993.

Splaine, John. *A Companion to the Lincoln Douglas Debates.* Washington, D.C.. National Cable Satellite Corporation, 1994.

Trefousse, Hans. *Andrew Johnson: A Biography.* W. W. Norton & Company, New York, NY. 1989.

The Boston Globe, 1872-1999.

The New York Times, 1860-1999.

The Washington Post, 1877-1999.

www.politicalgraveyard.com

http://starship.python.net/crew/manus

www.freep.com/news/inaug/trivia/index.htm

www.whitehouse.gov

Brian Lamb, founding CEO of C-SPAN, has been at the helm of the public affairs network since he helped the cable industry launch the first C-SPAN channel 31 years ago on March 19, 1979. In addition to visiting the gravesites of presidents and vice presidents, Brian has interviewed a number of living presidents—Nixon, Ford, Carter, Reagan, George H.W. Bush, Clinton, and George W. Bush. This is one of six books authored by Brian and the staff of C-SPAN including, most recently, *Abraham Lincoln: Great American Historians on our Sixteenth President.*

Presidential historian, author, lecturer, and speechwriter **Richard Norton Smith** has been the executive director of five presidential libraries (Hoover, Eisenhower, Reagan, Ford, and Lincoln) and of the Robert Dole Library in Kansas. He is currently a scholar-in-residence at George Mason University. Mr. Smith, shown here in front of a statue of Theodore Roosevelt on Roosevelt Island in Washington, D.C., has been a consultant to C-SPAN for several presidential history series.

Presidential historian and Rice University professor **Doug Brinkley** has written or edited more than two dozen books, including several presidential biographies. Mr. Brinkley has assisted with several C-SPAN projects, most recently serving as an advisor for C-SPAN's 2009 Survey on Presidential Leadership.

The C-SPAN networks were created as a public service by the cable industry to provide access to commercial-free coverage of the American political process. They are funded by their affiliates and receive no government or taxpayer support.

C-SPAN was launched in 1979 to provide live, gavel-to-gavel coverage of the U.S. House of Representatives. C-SPAN2 was created in 1986 to provide live, gavel-to-gavel coverage of the U.S. Senate. C-SPAN3, launched in 2001, provides additional choice in public affairs programming. The networks also offer other information and education services, including C-SPAN Radio, C-SPAN.org, C-SPAN Classroom and the C-SPAN Bus.

For more information, visit www.c-span.org.

To order C-SPAN videos, books, and educational products, visit www.c-span.org/shop or call 1–877-ONCSPAN.

All of C-SPAN's programming is archived at www.c-span.org.

C-SPAN®   **C-SPAN2®**   **C-SPAN3®**

C-SPAN RADIO   **C-SPAN CLASSROOM**   **C-SPAN.ORG**